CH/Mis

CLAIMING
the PROMISE

Can no longer be used in reading
program

1995 Education for Mission

CLAIMING
the PROMISE

African Churches Speak

Edited by
MARGARET S. LAROM

FRIENDSHIP PRESS · NEW YORK

Copyright © 1994 by Friendship Press, Inc.

Editorial Offices:
475 Riverside Drive, New York, NY 10115

Distribution Offices:
P.O. Box 37844, Cincinnati, OH 45222-0844

Manufactured in the United States of America

98   97   96   95   94   5   4   3   2   1

Library of Congress Cataloging-in-Publication Data

Claiming the promise : African churches speak / Musimbi Kanyoro...
[et al.].
    p. cm.
    ISBN 0-377-00267-4
    1. Christianity—Africa—20th century. 2. Africa—Church
history—20th century. 3. Theology, Doctrinal—Africa—
History—20th century. I. Kanyoro, Rachel Angogo, 1953- .
BR1360.C53 1994
276'.082—dc20   93-40417
                                                            CIP

Contents

Preface

The church in Africa is busy with the task of ministering to a continent that encompasses a great deal of diversity in language, nationality, ethnicity, and wealth. In the midst of such diversity it is often easier for outsiders to base their understanding of Africa on episodic events, which are all too often of a tragic and sensational nature, as opposed to the ongoing, everyday realities of life in Africa.

For those of us in the churches who want to deepen our understanding of Africa and the church in Africa, it is only natural that we should turn to our church partners in Africa for assistance. Such an effort holds great potential for enlarging our reservoir of spiritual resources and understanding of faithfulness.

The documents in this volume are the product of a dialogue in the church in Africa that is taking place at many different levels, involving individuals and organizations. The documents reflect issues of concern to the church in Africa as it struggles to identify the commonality of concerns emerging out of the diversity of Africa. This diversity holds the prospect of peril and promise. The churches, in their ministry, are busy claiming the promise of the gospel.

This book opens some windows for us on a continent full of faith and hope and struggle.

— WILLIS LOGAN, Director, Africa Office
National Council of the Churches of Christ in the USA

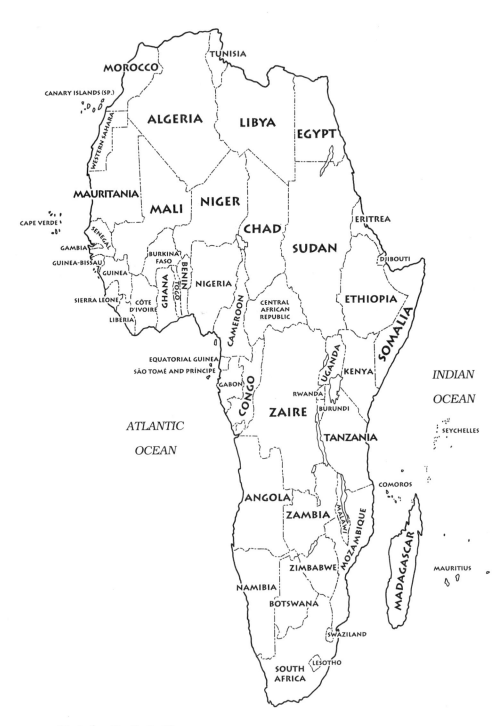

Map by Ruth Soffer

1

Christianity in Africa: Two Experiences

SILENCED BY CULTURE. SUSTAINED BY FAITH
Musimbi Kanyoro

I never talk about it. I recently asked myself, Why? Why do I keep it to myself? Why my silence on this particular issue?

I was the fourth daughter and the dividing line between expectant hope for the birth of a son and action to help the gods remedy a bad situation. My mother was considered the source of the bad situation—for it was claimed to be all her fault that she did not have male children. When I learned that my grandmother and aunts also despised my mother, I joined my three older sisters in being angry. Our anger was expressed in various ways; the most prominent was the lack of affection for these female relatives.

They didn't like us much either, so there was no love lost either way. We used "language" and silence to express this antagonism. They called us "immigrants," denoting that we would marry out of the clan, while privately we referred to them as the "auntilets"—showing their insignificance to us. We never came into direct confrontation, because culture does not allow minors to talk back to their seniors.

It is strange that even after so many years those feelings sometimes come alive and fill up my chest with heaviness. It is a burden that I have carried from the early years of my childhood, not finding a way to get rid of it. Neither can I claim that I even thought that it was necessary to get rid of it. However, the encounter with a women's perspective in theology has challenged me to reflect on this experience and to try to put it in perspective in relation to my faith.

Dr. Musimbi Kanyoro of Kenya is the secretary for Women in Church and Society, Lutheran World Federation, Geneva. This reflection is from a longer essay, "The Meaning of the Story: Theology as Experience," to be published in a forthcoming book edited by John Pobee on culture, women, and theology. Used by permission of John Pobee.

My Mother's Tears

Why did our aunts and grandmother, themselves women, give my mother such a tough time for giving birth to girls? What were the root causes of this behavior? The female members in the family found reasons not to be at peace with each other. The male members, on the other hand, chose not to be involved in "petty" matters and kept a safe distance from which they offered their love to the women in measures of their choosing.

My father, like others in my society, was bound by culture. He lived with the dilemma of longing to have sons, and even though he was well acquainted with medical facts and should have stood by my mother, he chose silence. While he never blamed her for giving birth to girls, he didn't protect her or us from the scorn and insults of his female relatives. We children loved him within bounds, treasuring his absence, which gave us freedom to be ourselves, and dreading his presence, which inhibited us. We thought we could read his unspoken words for each one of us, "I wish she was a boy," and his lamenting spirit, "Who will inherit my name and continue it to the generations to come?"

Throwing my mind's eye to those days of the past, I remember seeing my mother with tears in her eyes, especially late in the evening. She would do all the household chores, then she would see us through our school homework, and afterward she would go to the open verandah and cry. But she never explained the reason for her tears to us. Instead, if we joined her outside, she would stop crying and start singing. She would invent her own songs and sing them. They were mainly songs of hope. She would look far into the hills and sing her heart out. Then suddenly, life would come back—as if the hills had responded to her cry and were telling her, "I have heard the cry of my people." I remember one of her songs:

> Utahenda mwoyo mukivi
> Nyasaye arakurinda,
> Arakuretera busosi
> Nyasaye arakurinda.
>
> Yee, aarakurinda,
> mukiheri cha inzira,
> arakurinda hosi,
> Nyasaye arakurinda.

(Free translation: In whatever problems you have, you must not doubt or be anxious; God will take care of you. God will bring you rest. Yes, God will take care of you and protect you everywhere. God will take care of you.)

It was only when I became a teenager that I started to understand my mother's problems. I learned that her pain was based not only on the fact that we were girls but also on the uncertainty as to what we would grow up to be. One day, while doing homework with me, my mother put her hand around my shoulder and said: "My daughter, I want you to study hard. I want you to pass your examinations. If you fail your examinations, I will have failed."

But perhaps her most frequent source of sadness was the fear that we would choose or be lured into early marriage instead of an education and a career! The fears of raising girls in a society that valued boys constantly tormented her. Our safety from childhood to adult life was a load she had to bear as the mother of girls. Our failures would be blamed on her, while our successes would bring fame to our father and to the patrilineal clan system. Through all these worries, mother believed that God was still on her side.

Sustained by Faith

As I look back, I am amazed by my mother's consistency in her Christian faith. She prayed for us every day without fail. She prayed for each child by name. She read the Scriptures with us and sang the songs of the hymnal during such prayer sessions, but she composed her own songs when she was unhappy or extremely happy.

My mother read for us, mainly from the Psalms and the Gospels. She did not read for pleasure. Her busy schedule never had room for leisure reading. But she always found time to read the Bible. But why did she particularly prefer the Psalms and the Gospels?

Could it be that the Psalms depict the struggle of people and therefore invite us to identify with their message? The Psalms express the whole range of human emotions that are provoked in our response to God.

The Psalms are songs of faith in the living God, but it is often a faith that is born out of terrible pain and suffering. The Psalms bear witness to the truth that in all lamentation, in all supplication, and in all thanksgiving, we must ultimately confess that it is good to praise God, who is just and does justice with a view to our salvation. That my mother turned to Scriptures and chose the Psalms is a sign of her being sustained by faith. It is this message of faith that she wanted to pass on to her daughters, so that they too could look beyond culture to a God experience.

As she read the Psalms, she also sang songs. Through song, she joined others before her. She joined Myriam in Exodus 15 when she is said to have been suffering from leprosy but sang a praise song, full of hope and exaltation.

In the New Testament, the song of Mary, the Magnificat, has been highly exalted and volumes have been written about it. But what does the song mean to the suffering? We are reminded of the songs of the African slaves in America as they formed the freedom trail! Through song, they could communicate discretely as individuals, but also as a community. "We shall overcome! We shall overcome some day!" Or, "Oh, freedom, freedom over me!" Were these not the songs my mother was singing? She was not asking for political freedom, but freedom from an oppressive culture, freedom from a culture that had marginalized and silenced her as the mother of girls, a culture that had despised and silenced her own flesh and blood because of their gender. That she could turn to God could only have been by belief that God would not take sides with such a culture. The song of Mary, the exaltation of those of low degree, must have meant something for her. She strived to pass on that hope that comes through being sustained by faith.

The study of theology from the perspective of the oppressed has opened the eyes of many women who thought they were too blind to see theology, too deaf to hear it and understand it, too dumb to handle it, and too mute to articulate it. This type of theological reflection gives an imperative call to ordinary people to reflect on and interpret their experiences by articulating their thoughts and telling stories of their own journeys of faith.

CHURCHES FOR EVERYBODY: CHRISTIANITY IN NIGERIA
Modupe Oduyoye

In September 1992 the Methodist Church in Nigeria celebrated the 150th anniversary of Christianity in Nigeria, Thomas Birch Freeman of the Wesleyan Methodist Missionary Society having landed in Badagry on September 24, 1842. In that same year, the churches in my home town, Ijebu Ode, only about 150 kilometers away from Badagry, celebrated the centenary of Christianity in that town. The history of Christianity in Nigeria, then, is really very short: There are still second-generation Christians in many parts.

Roman Catholics will remind us that we are talking of the history of Protestantism. For just as Catholic priests accompanied Spanish conquistadors to Latin America beginning in 1492, so did Catholic chaplains follow Portuguese explorers along the coast of West Africa on their quest for a sea route to the Far East. Because Africa was nearer the Iberian peninsula than Latin America, the Catholics actually reached West Africa before 1492.

Reflections on the history of Christianity in Africa always include a warning: the fact that Christianity is widespread in Africa today does not guarantee that it will be popular forever. See what happened to the former Christian lands of North Africa, from Alexandria in Egypt to Hippo in present-day Algeria, when Islam came upon the scene. See what happened to the Christian land of Nubia, the country of the Eunuch of Ethiopia, the first non-Jew to receive baptism in the name of Jesus. That country is today the Islamic Republic of Sudan. The only trace left of the fifteenth-century Catholic mission in Warri and Benin City is the cassock and surplice design of the robes of kings and chiefs.

A Missionary Marshall Plan

European contact with West Africa from the fifteenth to the eighteenth centuries was dominated by the trans-Atlantic slave trade, which had such a deleterious effect on West Africa that militant Africans are even today demanding reparations. In fact, the European missionaries to West Africa in the nineteenth century paid reparations of a kind, for their policy of bringing the three Cs

---

Modupe Oduyoye is a noted writer, educator, linguist, editor, and publisher in Nigeria. He has been active in many Christian organizations and movements at the national, continental, and worldwide levels.

(Christianity, commerce, and civilization) to Africa involved sweeping away the slave trade through the establishment of "legitimate
trade." The Basel Mission founded what is today the United Trading
Company. The missionaries cooperated with the European trading companies to integrate Africa into the burgeoning European
capitalist international economic system. Unfortunately, this interest was appropriated by such incipient multinational companies as
the Royal Niger Company, which led the way for British colonial
appropriation of Nigeria from 1860 to 1960.

The history of Christianity in Nigeria is connected with the history of the abolition of the trans-Atlantic slave trade. This was a
fortunate connection. The gospel of redemption was both physical
(redemption from the slaveboat or from the slave plantations) and
metaphorical (redemption from the slavery of sin and the threat of
hell). The first-generation Christians were bound by ties of pleasant
memories to the new religion and those who brought it. These missionaries were as much dispensers of medicines as preachers of the
gospel of forgiveness. Their symbolic value was confused by the
intrusion of atheistic Europeans, who were from the same home
countries as the missionaries but who came to Africa on a different
mission — the partition of Africa as decided at the Berlin Conference of 1896, just fourteen years before the World Missionary
Conference in Edinburgh in 1910.

Within fifty years, "Ethiopian-type" churches had broken away.
They were called African churches, for example, the African Bap-
tist Church, the United African Methodist Church, the United Native
African Church, the African Church (Bethel) — all in Yoruba land.
And in another fifty years "Zionist-type" churches had sprung up:
the Christ Apostolic Church, the Cherubim and Seraphim, the Celes-
tial Church of Christ, the Church of the Lord–Aladura, the Precious
Stone Praying Band — all Pentecostal and African-instituted.

Thus from 1842 to about 1960 three types of churches were
established in Nigeria: the mission-founded churches, including Anglican, Methodist, Presbyterian, Salvation Army, Lutheran, Roman
Catholic, and Baptist; the African churches ("Ethiopian" and nationalist), which broke away from the mission-founded churches,
and the Aladura churches ("Zionist" and Pentecostalist). Since about
1960 the charismatic Christian fellowships have been added to this
list. These are the "yuppy" counterpart of the Aladura churches, often run by lay graduates, such as the Deeper Life Bible Church of
Nigeria, Scripture Pasture, and Christ Chapel.

A Church for Every Social Level

There is now no social class in Nigeria without a church to suit its level of formal schooling, income, and Westernization or indigenization. The problem of Christianity pulling Africans one way and African culture pulling them another no longer exists. There are now churches where the Westernized Nigerian can feel at home, with liturgy accompanied by the pipe organ played by an organist trained at the Royal College of Music, and there are churches where white-robed worshippers accompany their singing with hand clapping, drumming, and dancing.

The "Ethiopian"-type churches emancipated themselves from the missionary aversion to polygyny, asserting that polygyny was better than the repudiation of wives that the European missionaries prescribed as the only way to make former polygamists acceptable members of the church of Christ. While some still believe that monogamy is unnatural for the adult African male, the Roman Catholics in Africa are forging ahead with an invitation even to celibacy: the Bigard Memorial Seminary (in Enugu and Ikot Ekpene) is now the largest Catholic major seminary in the world. And while there are still male members of the mission-founded churches who practice secret polygyny, my father, a second-generation Christian, said to me: "I stand between you and a polygamous family life. If any one of you bypasses me to try and see what it is like, it will be his own responsibility." Although he was born into a household where his father, an adult convert to Christianity, had five wives and about twenty-two children, he had shielded us from that experience by having only one wife and four children. We had the experience of his brothers and cousins to observe for comparison. No Christian man in Nigeria today can boast in public of having more than one wife; it is no longer a measure of social achievement.

The cultural debates have been concluded. Nobody now asks me to leave the Cathedral Church of Christ, Marina, Lagos, because I am wearing dàṅṣíkí and not coat and tie; my baptismal name coincides with my Yoruba name Modupe, "I give thanks." My father was not compelled to pick a Hebrew name from the Bible. The drums are no longer banned from the church because they are branded as pagan.

One of the surest legacies of the mission-founded churches was the creation and sustenance of a Westernized elite in Nigeria. The majority of Westernized upper middle-class Nigerians who are members of the technocratic professions will be found in the mission-founded churches. Their self-employed counterparts will be found mainly in the "Ethiopian"-type churches: J. K. Coker, who led the secession from the Anglican Church in Lagos in 1891, was an apostle of cocoa plantation farming as well as a patron of the African church. These were the entrepreneurs who ensured that the missionary vision of self-support, self-government, and self-propagation was achieved in the Ethiopian and Zionist churches faster than in the mission-founded churches.

The Aladura churches were in the first generation essentially the churches of the working class; the worldview of its members is almost completely primal. Their enemies are identified as Satan and witches; their weapons are the name of Jesus and the names of God (El Shaddai, etc.); their champions in the fight are the angels (Michael, Gabriel, Raphael). Their analysis of sickness is exactly as in the New Testament: epilepsy is a result of demon possession, illness has spiritual causes, and faith-healing is so essential that in some cases any other type of healing is banned. Whereas mission-founded churches started and operated hospitals, the Aladura churches are run as an alternative system of medical care prescribing prayer and holy water—the water of salvation. Consulting a physician is considered evidence of insufficient faith in the power of Jesus; consulting a traditional diviner is considered anathema.

The mission-founded churches are faith and order churches, churches that have signed the Baptism, Eucharist, and Ministry Convention of the World Council of Churches; ministry in the Aladura churches is one of prophets and prophetesses. The ordination of women has never been a matter of debate in the Aladura churches.

Just as some of the sons and daughters of the clergy of the mission churches are emerging in the charismatic fellowships, so are some others emerging as "troublers of Israel" in the human rights movement. Ṣẹgun Ṣowunmi, recently retired professor of mathematics at the University of Ibadan, is chairman of the Nigerian chapter of Amnesty International. He and his wife, Bisi Ṣowunmi, professor of archaeology at the University of Ibadan, are children of Anglican clergy. She has just completed a seven-year term on the Central Committee of the World Council of Churches. Witness also the Ransome-Kuti brothers, sons of the Rev. I. O. Ransome-Kuti and grandchildren of the Rev. J. J. Ransome-Kuti, the singing minister of Ifọ, Abẹokuta. Professor Olikoye Ransome-Kuti has just completed a tenure of seven years as Nigeria's minister of health, during which he laid the foundations of the country's primary health care system. The other Kuti doctor, Beko, gets his passport seized every now and then by the security service, which keeps a dossier on his radical activities in the Civil Liberties Organization. And Fẹla Anikulapo-Kuti, an Afro-beat musician who dropped the "Ransome" in the hyphenated name of his grandfather to go back to the name of his ancestral family, abused the military with his song "Zombie" and got his house burned down by what the tribunal of enquiry concluded was the work of an "unknown soldier." About forty-five years ago their mother led the women of Abeokuta in a protest sit-in in front of the palace at Abeokuta; they kept the heat on until they learned that the *oba* had escaped into exile through a backdoor of the palace. He did not return to his throne for five years.

Christians and Society

Nevertheless, I see a lot of "soft-option" Christianity going on in Nigeria. The elite have been brought up to live as if they were in California. They join in criticizing what the affluent North is doing to the abject South but fail to see that this exploitation would be impossible without the collaboration they themselves supply through their aspirations for consumption. These products of the missionary program of Christianity, commerce, and civilization earn salaries as much as twenty times the wages of the lowest paid workers in the multinational companies of which they are the local managing directors. At the same time as the devaluation of the *naira* ruined further the purchasing capacity of the average Nigerian, satellite television dishes began to proliferate on the premises of the affluent. And many of them count themselves as part of the Christian population that must stem the tide of Islam.

I believe that the sects are instruments of lifting the hopeful poor. The hopeless poor patronize the beer parlor and the houses of drugs and prostitution and ruin themselves permanently, but the sects help the hopeful poor to preserve their dignity, and in twenty years these families and these sects become acceptable in society. There can be no better gauge of the degree of below-the-line existence in a society than the increase or decrease in the number of sects, which are problem-solving units not only for the founders but also for the members. Without these sects many people would live their lives as outcasts, unable to show their faces with dignity in places where only the well-dressed can feel at home, where you dare not arrive except in your own car.

The comfortable and the rich cannot understand this. They sit in their Sadducean churches and describe these sects as Pharisaic congregations of people who believe in angels and in spirits. The Seventh-Day Adventist Church, which recommends vegetarianism for its members, consequently frees them from the feeling of deprivation that comes from not being able to afford beef or chicken. When the grandchildren have made it they may move out of the sect, forgetting that their grandfathers could not have survived with their sanity without the ideological rejection of the food of the wealthy. The Celestial Church, which prohibits its members from entering the place of worship except barefooted, has solved a psychological problem for those members whose shoes are unpresentable on Sunday morning. They can spend their little earnings on absolute necessities of life and wait in hope until one of their children graduates from college.

There are thirty-six Anglican dioceses, but they have no publishing program. Activities of this kind have gone to the charismatic groups, and the bright young men and women are moving from the churches of the pipe organ and the grand piano to the churches of the electronic piano and desktop publishing. A lawyer has set up a branch of the Celestial Church in Badagry; an engineer is devoting more time to supplying the Celestial Church with organizational expertise; a young lecturer in physics has given up his university job to concentrate on running Scripture Pasture; a lecturer in mathematics gave up his job to run the Deeper Life Bible Church, which has become the church with the largest congregation in Nigeria; a retired professor of agriculture runs a congregation of the Celestial Church on his farm; a young teacher of chemistry is now the proprietor of Wisdom Books specializing in selling Christian books. We therefore have not only stories of churches that have become sedentary; we also have stories of vibrant pilgrim churches.

2

Problems and Promises of Africa: The Mombasa Symposium

André Karamaga

The All Africa Conference of Churches organized a symposium in 1991 on the problems and promises of Africa as the continent approaches the year 2000. Coming from 43 countries, the 184 participants met in November near Mombasa, the main coastal city of Kenya. The group included church executives, general secretaries of Christian councils, university professors, communicators, politicians, lay representatives, and ecumenical partners from all corners of the world. Many were women; some were youth.

The symposium, held at a time when Africa was experiencing changes and crises in many spheres, was timely as an opportunity for exchanging ideas and as a process of self-criticism urgently required if churches and countries of Africa are to survive.

New problems demand new solutions; the church as the servant of society is called upon to interpret the signs of the times. As Jesus affirmed, "new wine is put into fresh wineskins, and so both are preserved" (Matt. 9:17).

Most missionary societies making their appearance in Africa during the eighteenth and nineteenth centuries had been founded by the various denominations. In 1910, when these societies met at Edinburgh, they failed to overcome their divisions to present a unified message to Africa in keeping with the Gospel of John 17:21. To the contrary, many churches in Africa were established precisely along both denominational and ethnic lines, thereby negatively reinforcing the natural diversities of Africa. In 1939, when Western churches and mission societies were confronted by the peril of global conflict and World War II, they came together to

The Rev. Dr. André Karamaga of Rwanda is the program officer for the AACC Information and Theology Desk. This essay is condensed from a summary of the AACC Symposium in Mombasa in November 1991 and published as *Problems and Promises of Africa: Towards and Beyond the Year 2000.* © 1991 All Africa Conference of Churches. Used by permission.

pool common resources. However, when the war ended, the spirit of denominationalism was revived in full strength.

In 1948, the World Council of Churches was created on a denominational basis; in 1963, when the All Africa Conference of Churches was formed, it also was unable to avoid the dynamic of denominationalism. Is not this the time to declare an end to the era of imported denominations? The Christian movement in Africa must be deeply renewed if it is to inspire the process of transformation and if it is to fulfill the hopes for freedom and democracy being expressed across this continent.

Furthermore, the widespread misery experienced across Africa is a flagrant contradiction of theological significance that the church must address. Indeed, how can it be explained that this deeply religious continent is also the continent in which people are the most exploited? Could it be said that the fear of the Lord is the beginning of misery rather than the beginning of wisdom (see Ps. 111:10)? It is precisely this issue that links the deliberations of the symposium to the theme of the Sixth General Assembly of the AACC, namely, "Abundant Life in Jesus Christ" (John 10:10).

In addition to papers prepared by specialists from a variety of disciplines, the symposium dealt with several major topics in interest groups. The six themes were:

Group I   The Church of the Future in Africa
Group II   Rethinking Our Social and Political Structures
Group III Culture and Development
Group IV   Secularism and Religious Pluralism
Group V   Church Unity and the Unity of Humanity
Group VI   Communication and Witness

This report summarizes the issues dealt with in each group as well as those questions that remain open as an invitation to further study.

The Church of the Future in Africa

It is high time to recognize God's gifts of innovation and creativity. Ecclesial institutions and structures exist to meet the needs of human beings and of society generally. When church institutions function like islands, harboring elements of divisiveness, they become instruments of alienation.

Equipped as we are with our denominational structures, there is a temptation to rely more on such structures than on God. As human beings, we long for continuity, forgetting that at times God acts through discontinuity and change.

Symposium participants understood that they need no longer be bound by slavish obedience to the past, but must instead be open to the guidance of the Holy Spirit and to the concerns of the people of God. Rather than concentrating on the "Future of the Church," Group I decided to focus on the "Church of the Future"—the former being preoccupied with existing structures and denominations and the latter suggesting openness to innovation and creativity.

The Need for Radical Change

The church as an institution cannot be isolated from the upheavals currently assaulting the world generally and Africa in particular. God the Creator is involved in a process of continuous innovation. When it is said that Jesus is the same yesterday, today, and forever (Heb. 13:8), it should also be remembered that God's word is new to each generation and to each context.

As God's instrument, the church is called to participate prophetically on the cutting edge of world events. Across the continent the guidance and mediation of churches have been sought by politicians and by the general public to address the current sociopolitical crises. In this context, Group I highlighted the church's most serious weakness: "The churches in Africa have never fully shouldered their responsibilities and are still considered as perpetual children. At the end of the twentieth century, following the missionary era, we still find it difficult to conceive and to implement what we should do by ourselves. We give only lip-service to autonomy, and church members do not seem to give importance to it."

The dependence of our communities has implications for the maturity of the people of God, especially in areas of theological discernment, finance, and personnel. It is abnormal to be waiting for financial and program assistance from overseas churches. It is sinful to surrender our power, our thoughts, and our action initiatives to overseas partner churches. If we are to participate fully in the universality of the church, we must mobilize our own resources and become conscious of who we are as the church in Africa.

The Ecumenical Partners' Working Group cited this new awareness when they reported: "We have noted a strong willingness to achieve self-determination and self-sufficiency. Numerous statements and constructive criticism confirm the impressions that Africans now seriously intend to control their own affairs. This intention goes together with a re-evaluation of African values and an awareness of past failures."

Such a shift in awareness also implies a reshaping of basic norms. The time has come for churches to distance themselves from outdated conservatism. Our disciplinary regulations and our conceptions of the ministry that discriminate against women must be seriously reconsidered. We still cling to structures, doctrines, liturgy, rules, and regulations that are not of our own making. Often we insist on maintaining outdated practices that are no longer observed even in the countries of origin. Nineteenth-century hymns passed on to us by the missionaries still rank high in African church communities. Has the invitation to "sing to the Lord a new song" (Ps. 96:1) fallen on deaf ears in Africa? Does not our cultural heritage contain rich musical resources that could be energized by the churches?

If the church refuses to take the initiative toward the transformation of our times, then the changes already under way in the larger world community will have a negative impact on the church's image and mission.

A Church Open to All

Group I noted that the church tends to exclude or marginalize especially women, youth, and the handicapped. In his opening remarks to the symposium, the general secretary of the AACC, the Rev. José Belo Chipenda, evoked similar concerns: "The church is made up of all the social groups found in any society: children, young people, young couples, women, men, senior citizens, single parents, the handicapped, and strangers in our midst. A successful Christian program must meet the physical, moral, and spiritual needs of all these groups, starting with children. Any church that does not have an attractive children and youth program is doomed to failure."

Children are sidelined because of cultural taboos in African traditions, noted Group I. Children and young people are expected to listen to and learn from the elders; they are not expected to interrupt an adult discussion. This expectation does not correspond to the teaching of the gospel.

Women expressed concern about their own exclusion: "If it is true that women are the majority in the church, then they form a dynamic force in the church and their problems and concerns should be catered to. Women fear that the popular word 'democracy' might become meaningless for them because the structures of several churches are undemocratic. As in the family and society in general, is the church also the domain of men?"

African women are victims of isolation in the home, at work, and even in the church. Formal education for girls as well as women's programs in the churches train for domestic duties rather than for participation in modern life. Women's groups in our churches function as development constraints, especially to women intellectuals, because of conservative and outdated educational methods.

The Laity interest group expressed a similar concern: "We constitute the majority of church members but we often play passive roles. We do not always participate in decision-making on matters concerning us. This makes us less devoted to the church."

Group I recommended that changes be made in the decision-making process, management structure, and service delivery mechanisms within the church, inviting the participation of all children, youth, women, the laity, the disabled, and the clergy with each contributing according to their gifts and skills.

The Church of the Future should not divide people into categories but should unite everyone for a common witness. It should not be controlled exclusively by any group; rather it should function as a fellowship in which everyone blossoms and finds hope. Such a church should be open not only to its immediate members but to society as a whole.

Toward a New Theological Foundation

Speaking on the situation of the churches in Africa, the general secretary used a metaphor: "African churches are at the crossroads, between the promises of the future and problems with very grave implications. When one considers these problems in isolation from other matters, one is certain to be overwhelmed by despair. However, if one considers the promises, they lead one to hope."

The crossroads metaphor surfaced repeatedly at the symposium, signaling the need to make courageous decisions. It was as if God were repeating an Old Testament admonition to African churches: "I call heaven and earth to witness against you today that I have set before you life and death, blessings and curses. Choose life so that you and your descendants may live" (Deut. 30:19).

If the church is to choose life, commitments on the basis of careful reflection must be made. However, in Africa there is the tendency to begin with action. In the Church of the Future, theological reflection is of primary importance because the church cannot grow in a vacuum. It needs a strong biblical, theological foundation on which to base its programs, projects, and witness.

Jesse Mugambi of Kenya stated that the key terms in African Christian theology for the twenty-first century should be "reconstruction" and "social transformation." During the 1960s and 1970s, African theology emphasized liberation, which was then necessary for extrication from colonial servitude, but it was relatively silent on the need for social transformation and reconstruction.

The church needs Christians with strong faith supported by a thorough knowledge of the gospel in order to witness for Christ. Reliance on Sunday sermons for this purpose is not sufficient. The church needs group leaders, deacons, and elders with a sound knowledge of the biblical message to enhance the quality of their ministry. Pastors who already have received theological training should be trained to sustain interaction and dialogue with everyone, especially the youth. Parents also need training to carry out Christian family education.

The present classical training in theology is based on a hierarchical pyramid in which pastors are trained first with the expectation that they in turn train lay members of the church. Community education, however, focuses on all of God's people in the church and is carried out by trainer teams comprising both lay members and pastors. The training should be held in parishes, lay training centers, seminars, and Bible study at the local level.

Toward a Missionary Church

Participants at the symposium considered the Church of the Future from the perspective of the missionary imperative, that is, a church committed to participating in God's dynamic action in the world.

Surprisingly, Africa is still regarded as a mission field. Certain missionary societies seem not to be aware of the new situation. New missionary groups are still organizing themselves in Europe and North America to establish Christian missions in Africa, apparently still considered to be the "pagan" continent.

The truth is that the African church represents a majority of the people in Africa today—and this at a time when Europe and America are experiencing a process of "de-Christianization." If African churches are to reconceptualize their missionary task, they will need to assume responsibility for a witness on the African continent. If missionary societies are genuinely concerned about adapting to the new situation, they must now act in concert with Africans toward new structures and a multidirectional mission process, replacing the old one-way mission pattern.

The symposium in Mombasa noted the temptation of the church to consider itself the center of everything. Indeed, the meeting was characterized by phrases such as "the church must," "the church should" or "the church can," as if the church were a self-sufficient center. We must become aware of our constraints, realizing that the church can do nothing without the Lord Jesus Christ.

Rethinking Our Social and Political Structures

In African society, the family constitutes the central component. For family is the space in which life is lived, in which rights are claimed and exercised. The dimensions of family vary from place to place, often extending beyond the basic nucleus of father, mother, and children. In traditional Africa, the family played an educator role, preparing the young for adult life. It was the place, more than any other, in which solidarity, communion, and interdependence were experienced.

Today, this traditional framework has given way to a new world in which the disintegration of the extended family is apparently irreversible. This phenomenon can be understood in the context of the rural-to-urban exodus, in the variety of educational demands, and in general population movements.

These changes are associated with the general weakening of the social structure within which marriage has traditionally played an important role. When today's young people begin making decisions about establishing their families, typically parents are no longer involved. The upbringing of children suffers when the respective roles of parents, the schools, and the church are either unclear or confused. The current fluid situation requires continuing reflection and clarification from the church.

Can the church really replace the family in the moral and religious education of children? Even if the church has today assumed the duty of counseling and advising individuals and couples—a duty traditionally exercised by the extended family—it cannot claim to replace the nuclear family as far as social education is concerned. In fact, much would be gained by establishing educational responsibilities at every level of the extended family. In this way, the very foundation of African society would function at once as the foundation of the church of the future.

As long as schools are state-controlled and state-administered, they cannot provide an integrated education for children. State-administered schools provide book knowledge, which to a greater or lesser extent creates distance between children and parents. Thus children acquire extensive knowledge about modern life while the parents retain the cultural heritage and wisdom that their off-spring need for spiritual growth and development.

The church has the duty to prepare parents for the irreplace-able task of educating their children. Furthermore, the dialogue among the three partners involved in education—the family, the school, and the church—is both indispensable and complementary. The church should pay special attention to marriage, still the most appropriate institution for the development of children, and wage a relentless struggle against the negative influences coming from countries where the marriage contract facilitates only a temporary coexistence.

However, it must also be recognized that for one reason or other, some people do not marry. Such people should be made to feel at home within the church. Celibacy also must be accorded due value.

If the church plays the role of the extended family, it should con-stantly be mindful of children who are not blessed with the care of a natural family. Children are being orphaned by AIDS while others are abandoned from birth. All such children are entitled to atten-tion, affection, guidance, and counseling from society and from the extended family, the church. Equally affected are the aged and other marginalized people who do not benefit from anyone's care as a result of the disintegration of the extended family.

Concerning population growth—a favorite donor theme—Burk-ina Faso's Professor Joseph Ki-Zerbo noted, "In the North, Africa's population 'explosion' is perceived as the source of all ills whereas it should be considered as the result of other factors. The fertility rate of 6.6 per woman has not changed since 1965 in a number of African countries. And this is due to a whole range of economic, psychological, sociological, religious, and political motivations."

What is being witnessed is not some bestial irresponsibility, but deliberate behavior informed by the strongest motivations to live and survive. However, Professor Ki-Zerbo also stressed that Africa's population growth cannot be unlinked from the continent's specific economic conditions. "Fifty percent of Africa's population consists of young people below fifteen years of age. In the next thirty years, up to the year 2020, there will be 350 million new job-seekers."

According to Professor Ki-Zerbo, the provision of millions of contraceptives is not the best way to achieve a healthy population balance. Instead, education that cautions against early marriages and that supports improvement in family living standards would produce better results. Christians should be the first to understand that the act of producing children who can be neither properly nurtured nor adequately educated is simply irresponsible and criminal.

Democracy

Today Africans are living in a period of confusion, strongly influenced by the bankruptcy of imported ideologies. Neither Marxism, now on its deathbed, nor capitalism, busy celebrating the demise of its rival, has proven helpful to African countries trying to escape political stagnation.

The reality is that capital-starved Africa cannot possibly benefit from the capitalist game nor can it play the capitalist game by international rules. Today the continent's real capital consists of peasant masses who have been in a centuries-long struggle for survival. How will these masses be given the attention they deserve as long as Africa continues in its internationally subordinate position? The answer lies in the quest for genuine freedom and democracy being pursued by people across the continent.

However, it cannot be assumed that democracy is everywhere understood in Africa. Democracy is defined as government by the people, as the encouragement of free expression, dialogue, and participation by all in the management of their respective countries. In true democracy, diverse ideas within a given community are taken into account and respected in an open, transparent atmosphere.

Any democracy that served as handmaiden of the colonial enterprise is unworthy of emulation by Africa. Africans aspire to democracy that brings freedom and self-determination with dignity. Such freedom is genuine only if it incarnates the values of justice and tolerance. A democracy suited to Africa should reinforce the cultural values of community life, guarding against individualistic tendencies. The democratic ideal will be realized in our countries when inclusivist systems bring us together, encouraging a community of harmonious sharing.

Although Africans themselves may be oblivious to the reality, the lack of freedom is in fact very costly for the African continent. Who does not feel anguish when African intellectuals are forced into exile in Europe or North America? These intellectuals have been accused of staying abroad after studies or going into exile only to earn big salaries. While some of the most brilliant ones are indeed recruited into lucrative jobs, others in Europe or in North America are constantly subjected to humiliation, making do with jobs not at all commensurate with their level of expertise or training. They tolerate the situation only because it offers relative peace and some degree of free expression.

Still other African intellectuals return to their native lands only to find themselves disappointed and frustrated by oppressive regimes. They maintain intellectual integrity by avoiding establishment positions and are frequently destined to end their days in prison or in exile. On the other hand, Africa is a dream continent for many foreigners. Those with the opportunity to live and work on the continent leave reluctantly upon completion of their contracts. It is therefore a supreme irony that Europeans and North Americans fill positions left vacant by Africa's own sons and daughters who experience "home" as insecure and frustrating, as a place to avoid if they are to have peace of mind.

Group 3 reminded churches that the best way to encourage democracy is to set an example: "Our churches, just like our societies, have patriarchal structures which marginalize women, the youth, and children. As long as a church's structures remain undemocratic, this same church will not be able to denounce the absence of democracy in the governmental structure."

Security and Human Rights

Some African states are signatories to the Charter of Human and Peoples' Rights, and many claim to uphold fundamental human rights. But with the tragedy of famine, with children living in the streets of our cities, it becomes apparent that flagrant violation of human rights is in fact pervasive. Everyone, including the church, has become accustomed to living with these problems and accepting them as integral to the African condition. Foreign human rights associations are preoccupied with the cruelty in African countries related to imprisonment, torture, or even physical liquidation. But they often fail to take note of the misery and deprivation of everyday life as unacceptable violations of human rights.

Ironically, these evils are rarely denounced from within African countries themselves, not even by the churches or by other humanitarian organizations. It is high time that Africans question this state of affairs, rearticulating the most appropriate and acceptable means of achieving justice.

Generally speaking, Africans lay claim to cultures characterized by respect for life. Traditional justice did not require culprits to be tortured or physically eliminated. In some societies, interrogations were conducted in the form of a respectful dialogue with the suspect. Other ethnic groups used medicines that persuaded the accused to admit guilt. These methods were intended only to reveal the truth in a humane fashion. Values of this kind should not be forgotten or neglected.

Redefining Priorities

The archbishop of Cape Town, Desmond Tutu, current president of the AACC, has repeatedly insisted that "peace is cheaper than repression." Indeed, the decision by any country, whether rich or poor, to engage in war is also a decision to assign a great portion of its resources—human, material, and financial—to a destructive enterprise. During the last three decades, African countries have devoted substantial resources to the purchase of military equipment, ostensibly for defense. And yet this kind of investment has yielded only a rich harvest of *coups d'état* and self-destruction.

Africa's armies, established and equipped at great cost, have impoverished our people; they have not fought Africa's real enemies of poverty, insecurity, famine, and illiteracy. On the contrary, they frequently have been used to suppress and silence the very people who pay for them.

Ongoing civil wars, which destroy property and human lives, benefit only arms dealers. The continent's most miserable countries are those that have been most ravaged by civil war. When Africans opt for peace, they will save large sums of money that can be applied to other priority areas such as education.

The Refugee Phenomenon

It is impossible to talk about human rights and a rethinking of African structures without considering the chronic refugee problem on this continent. The people of Africa have suffered so much at the hands of non-Africans that they should be the first to understand the pain inflicted by aggression. What is the meaning of the oft-praised values of tolerance and respect, claimed as the foundation of African culture, if in fact individuals and groups of people are being hounded out of their motherlands?

The refugee phenomenon (the number of refugees on the African continent today exceeds six million) developed under our very eyes as our countries became independent. For refugees, independence has been forfeited by their own exile while the right to human dignity has been denied.

The refugee phenomenon is rendered even more complex by an additional fourteen million "displaced people," who stay within the boundaries of their own countries, but because of war or famine abandon their homes. Because of the nature of current refugee legislation, displaced people are essentially ignored while properly recognized refugees are provided with humanitarian assistance. Speaking for the symposium group that examined this phenomenon, Canon Kodwo E. Ankrah of Ghana and Uganda, said, "Africa's borders are both irrational and inappropriate and have been a constant source of civil wars and regional conflicts. The refugee phenomenon in Africa has come about simply because political and economic situations in Africa have deteriorated. As long as our churches remain silent about these causes, they remain accomplices of the crimes committed by the states against the people."

Culture and Development

No nation or community can develop without clear rootedness in its past. Immediately before and after independence, Africans clearly understood the need to re-examine their culture and to assert a new identity. But this search was undermined by the imposition of foreign ideologies onto newly independent African countries, which provided the cornerstone for subsequent developments in Africa.

At present, Africans face a dilemma. We are not sure whether to retreat for a re-examination of our own culture or to march forward on the basis of foreign cultures. The dilemma is rendered even more intense by our inability to take clear positions on the manner in which our futures are determined. For example, political, military, and multinational economic powers are pursuing geopolitical strategies that plunge Africa ever deeper into debt and into chronic dependence on the industrialized world.

Today Africans are like people lost in a vast jungle without understanding the management rules of the jungle. They are either unable or unwilling to reshape their traditional world vision, and they are not at home in the new, artificial world that operates without their participation and not at all in their favor.

By which process should our present culture and identity be re-examined? A Zairian proverb says that a piece of wood can stay in the water for centuries without turning into a crocodile, i.e., we have survived and retained the core of our African identity despite bitter experience, false starts, and directions lost.

Prophets of doom, who either fail to appreciate our dynamism or shrink back in fear of it, take advantage of the African crisis to suggest that we are forever lost. But the future has much in store for those who continue in hope. Even though much has been lost, we have retained the core of what makes us African. Hope and the determination to live, the pillars of our culture, have enabled the deprived people of Africa to struggle and survive against innumerable odds. Even when struck by forces and disasters beyond their control, no amount of tribulation has destroyed the Africans' determination to always begin afresh.

Cultural Alienation

Our African identity is the internal force and dynamism that has helped Africans to survive despite the atrocities of slavery, colonization, and postcolonial dictatorships. This "Africanness" helped African-Americans retain their humanity and endure the inhuman treatment unleashed on them for centuries. Nevertheless, the threat of alienation still haunts us.

The Mombasa Symposium noted the seriousness and depth of our cultural crisis. What remains of our Africanness should not be regarded as a static force meant simply to ensure our survival. It should rather act as a springboard, enabling us to take a leap forward beyond the present status quo. If that leap is to be made, alienation with all its implications and symptoms must be assessed.

A primary symptom is a lack of confidence in our own abilities. Hence the search for assistance to acquire what could easily be obtained on our own. We are caught up in a vicious circle of begging. Thus we thank foreigners for assistance even when the content of such assistance was originally robbed from our continent.

With regard to culture, the symptoms of alienation are best exemplified by the African ruling elite who try constantly to introduce European or American lifestyles into our countries and by the current television and radio programs beamed into many African countries. What is the purpose of a national radio or television network that does not give priority to the production and broadcasting of local programs?

Some African countries have signed what are known as cultural cooperation agreements with foreign countries. The pictures and sounds from foreign radio and television stations give Africans the sense of being strangers in their own country. The Mombasa Symposium condemned such alienating cultural imperialism and recommended that churches and all Africans of good will act to check this trend.

With regard to the use of English, French, and Portuguese, the symposium noted that these languages are still required to facilitate communication within Africa and with the rest of the world. However, their use should not be permitted to act as a wedge to divide and separate African people and countries to the advantage of foreign powers.

Another glaring example of cultural alienation in Africa is the tendency to accept mediocre work; we subconsciously have accepted the bias held by foreigners who believe that an African is incapable of doing anything well. We are strongly convinced that goods produced by Africans are not worth buying.

Many academicians still consider the Christian church in Africa as a powerful outpost of Western imperialism, functioning at the expense of African cultures. Indeed, the church must constantly assess the nature of the relationship between the gospel and culture.

Gospel and Culture

What causes Africans to take the gospel seriously? The gospel is an invitation to salvation, and a response to the invitation releases people from the bondage of the status quo. Salvation concerns human life in Africa, the very life that is threatened from within and without. It is the life about which Jesus spoke in John 10:10.

Life, which is the ultimate goal of the gospel, is also the major concern of African cultures; it provides the cornerstone of the spirituality of most African people. The gospel is an unequaled force in promoting life—a bountiful life, not only after death but also here on earth. When people who believe in God, the giver of life, are subjected to untold misery and alienation, the inculturation of the gospel is at risk.

Certainly this vision of the relationship between the gospel and culture has implications for the way people regard the church and for the way Christians behave. Our daily struggle against the forces of death should be based on actions inspired not only by basic survival instincts, but by a deep faith in God, the giver of life. Professor Mugambi says, "No church can withstand history's challenge if it does not embrace the gospel within the cultural and religious heritage of each generation."

Therefore, the basic question is not, "What is the nature of African identity when permeated by the gospel?" but rather, "How does the gospel enrich our identity and transform people into Africans worthy of the name?" Surely the original purpose of the gospel is not intended to uproot people culturally, but rather to strengthen and consolidate their identity.

Cooperation Worse Than Colonialism

During the slave trade period, Africans were chained with iron chains, which they could feel and easily associate with their suffering. Colonization was a system of direct domination from which the colonizers benefited. The postcolonial era, wrongly referred to as the era of cooperation, is worse than colonization. Africans are once again chained, but this time by "cooperation agreements."

The independence movement of the 1960s spread like bushfire. Africans thought they would be free to control their own destiny and would witness a new era of freedom and self-determination. Unfortunately, the colonial powers established strategies to manipulate the new situation, quickly consolidating their advantage and domination over Africa. They assisted in the formation of strong regimes. Any opposition was eliminated as a prerequisite for attracting foreign investment and capital. Thus were single-party regimes established in most African countries.

The former colonial powers signed agreements stipulating that export earnings of supposedly independent African states should be controlled. In exchange for such measures, the dominant foreign powers would guarantee currency values. Obviously, such agreements gave the central banks of the guarantor countries power to exercise monopoly control over all significant monetary transactions. What remains of the independence of a country that cannot formulate or control its own economic and monetary policy?

Military agreements had similar effects. Careful scrutiny reveals that real power resides in the embassy of the former colonial power rather than with the local leaders. Typically, the ambassador of the foreign power has the exclusive authority to call in military units from his country without the consent of the local authorities.

Generally, cultural agreements are lopsided, designed to ensure the establishment and maintenance of cultural centers and television and radio networks that promote the cultural and political interests of foreign powers. This type of cooperation renders independence hollow and meaningless.

Economic Structural Adjustment Programs dictated by the same foreign powers are relegating Africa to the periphery and ensuring that it remain there. Structural Adjustment Programs have forced African countries to increase exports in order to generate more foreign currency to finance debts, some of which were incurred under dubious circumstances. The debt factor is one of the most absurd aspects of the relationship between Africa and the superpowers, who know all too well that Africa is exporting more money than it receives by way of aid or remuneration for commodities. Furthermore, the terms governing debt repayment and the pace at which interest on the debt increases together ensure that Africa's debt will never be repaid.

Hope Is Not Lost

The symposium's working groups, examining the African situation openly and pragmatically, concluded that Africa's performance has in many aspects been very poor indeed. However, the symposium did not yield to pessimism and fatalism, but identified new perspectives for discussion at the national level.

As Rev. Chipenda says, "If Africa is to face the future realistically, the word 'development' must be revisited and the cultural dimensions of life emphasized much more than in the past. There will be no future for the majority of our people without serious appreciation of God's religio-cultural gifts to Africa."

All participants agreed that an atmosphere of peace, security, and stability is a prerequisite for genuine development. To establish and promote such an atmosphere, capital investment is in fact necessary—but so is political will based on the belief that war and repression are avoidable, destructive activities. Therefore, the democratization process taking place in Africa today must be taken seriously. As long as people are denied freedom and the right to express different opinions, we will continue to witness violent clashes. Today it is easy to use physical violence because of the proliferation of firearms in all African countries.

With regard to the debt problem, Rev. Chipenda recommended that by 1995 a jubilee should be proclaimed: "Without a moratorium on the repayment of existing debts, there will be no happy future for Africa's children." Furthermore, cooperation should be reviewed to enable Africans to benefit from their resources and efforts instead of merely continuing to serve foreign interests. Churches have the important role of sensitizing the rural masses to their rights or denouncing mistakes made in the management of the African countries.

Ecumenical representatives pledged to cooperate with African churches in all their commitments and requested them to "take full advantage of the possibilities that the partners have to criticize the economic and political setups and any other interests of the North which have a negative impact on Africa."

Many experts at the Mombasa Symposium felt that Africa should have the courage to disengage itself from the world economy and set up its own market. However, smooth and concrete development can be realized only if development efforts take into account the wisdom and potential of the rural masses.

Secularism and Religious Pluralism

There are three main religions in Africa, namely, traditional religion, Islam, and Christianity. All three claim adherents throughout the whole of Africa and all acknowledge and worship a single, transcendent God. In other words, all three are monotheist, although in contrast to Islam and Christianity, African traditional religion does not have a sacred book.

African religious expression is not a recent phenomenon. Its roots can be traced to time immemorial. It has been claimed that Africans are "an incurably religious people." Anyone seeking to understand the role and the consequences of religious belief in African society must face the question, "Does religious belief as practiced in Africa share some responsibility for the prevalence and persistence of calamities all over the continent?"

In many African countries, according to 1990 UN figures, life expectancy at birth is only 51 years, compared to 62 in other developing countries and 74 in the industrialized countries. More than 50 percent of all Africans have no access to medical care, while 63 percent of the population in other developing countries enjoy adequate medical care. In some industrialized countries, medical care covers 100 percent of the population. In most of Africa, malnutrition, widespread famine, and illiteracy are becoming entrenched rather than resolved.

Recent forecasts predict that the countries and populations of this continent are ensnared by a process that will take them from poverty to utter destitution. Yet Africa is labeled as one of the most religious continents in the world. Christianity, long considered an imported religion, continues its remarkable expansion. Estimates indicate that every day up to 16,000 Africans embrace the Christian faith. Professor Jesse Mugambi focuses the issues: "How could it be that peoples who continue to call on God most reverently are the ones whom God seems to neglect most vehemently? Could it be that irreligion is the key to success and that religion is the key to backwardness? It is paradoxical that those nations in which Christianity is supposedly declining, and some in the Orient, where Christianity has never made a significant impact, are the ones that are economically prosperous. Apparently it is necessary to cast religion aside, and the ethic associated with it, in order to build a viable economy."

Symposium participants faced these challenges with a critical reflection on Christian theology and its consequences. All three religions, soliciting either allegiance or members within the African community, preach salvation and well-being. None would admit to playing negative roles in African life or deliberately acting as instruments of alienation or foreign domination.

The Christian gospel is a source of liberation and renewal, capable of transforming the profile and the conditions of any country and any people. Just as Jacob said when he was wrestling with God, "I will not let you go, unless you bless me" (Gen. 32:26), Africans cling to God in order to enjoy God's blessing. A religion without blessing and without a liberating dynamic is what Karl Marx termed the "opiate of the people."

The Various Christian Groups

Until now, the continent has been considered by foreigners as an area still open to religious proselytism. Among both Christian and Muslim evangelists there is the mistaken belief that Africans have no religion of their own or that they readily succumb to new religions. Some missionaries exploit the poverty and vulnerability of African peoples, enticing them with financial or material gifts.

New Zealand–born theologian Paul Gifford analyzed the impact of various Christian movements on the present and future of African peoples. "These new groups are not all identical and interchangeable. But there are recognizable emphases that are associated with these groups, their crusades, rallies, Bible colleges, Bible courses, conferences, pastors' workshops, and sermons."

Most of the fundamentalist movements active in Africa exploit the fears and insecurity of people by emphasizing the apocalyptic character of the present times. They claim that the difficulties and distress experienced today are but the fulfillment of biblical prophesies. As famine or poverty become more intense, God's promised deliverance comes ever closer.

It is easy to calculate the sociopolitical impact of such a debilitating theology. It claims that impoverishment, the status quo, and chaos are manifestations of God's will. Those facing such situations need not engage in a struggle to extract themselves; instead they should expect tribulation in this life and salvation in life hereafter. The Christian's role is simply to believe in Jesus and to wait patiently for his return.

These sectarian movements blame all evil on Satan and the evil spirits, an attitude that diverts attention from the political or economic sources of local or national problems. Do Christians have any right to place their own foibles and irresponsible acts on Satan's doorstep? Is genuine trust toward God and Jesus Christ, our Lord and Brother, not a matter of addressing evil by addressing and resolving illness, famine, war, and alienation?

Religious Diversity

Not everyone in Africa agrees that religion makes a positive contribution to peace and harmony. On the contrary, religion is viewed as a time bomb that could ignite and sustain conflicts. Religion as a source of conflict has been introduced into Africa by Islam and Christianity. Traditional African religion was devoid of any fanaticism, rivalries, and wars waged in the name of God; it saw God as a powerful entity who did not require the armed defense of believers. Indeed, the armed defense of God was considered by traditional religion as a sin, reducing the Supreme Being to the rank of an idol requiring protection from human beings.

Both Christianity and Islam would do well to consider the wisdom from traditional religion. Meanwhile, conflicts have become a reality even within some Christian groups.

The Mombasa Symposium gave special attention to the burning issue of Muslim-Christian relationships, after a presentation by Dutch theologian Johannes Haafkens, who has undertaken extensive research on this subject in recent years as part of the Project for Christian-Muslim Relations in Africa (see below, pp. 108–116).

Reactions varied considerably. Participants from countries where Islam is the minority religion seemed to minimize the problem and condemned any form of fanaticism by Christians or Muslims.

On the other hand, participants from predominantly Muslim countries were quite hesitant to enter into open relationships with Islam; they were ready instead to identify strategies that would help Christians face the perceived threat of Islamic militancy. Whether Christian or Muslim, people throughout the region still adhere to remnants of traditional belief, which advocates tolerance as an important religious tenet.

Traditional religion provides an avenue through which African Christianity and Islam can harmonize their relationships. Because of its deep-rooted links with culture and its denial of any dichotomy between the sacred and secular, the influence of traditional religion continues. Some scholars estimate that 80 percent of sub-Saharan Africans are practicing adherents of traditional religions despite their outward allegiance to Christianity or Islam.

In its encounter with traditional religion, Christianity has always pointed to the dangers of syncretism with its blending and fusing of diverse or opposing religious traditions. However, at the Mombasa Symposium, no one even mentioned the word. It is possible that Africans do not view syncretism as a serious threat, since they are convinced that all major religions represent an admixture of concepts and elements with diverse origins. Religious tolerance is one of the values that the traditional religionist brings to the unity of faith.

Church Unity and the Unity of Humanity

Group V of the Mombasa Symposium examined the question: "Is unity, whether of the church or humankind, a necessity in contemporary Africa?" Everywhere there are indications of many kinds of painful divisions.

Because of the nature of geographic, racial, or linguistic population distributions in Africa, past discussions focused on "differences" rather than on inequalities and thus on divisions. People from one region impose hegemony on another people, thus redefining or marginalizing a legitimate people. Some races and languages enjoy privileged positions at the expense of others, enforcing unacceptable concessions and causing deep frustration. It is precisely the most privileged in today's economically imbalanced and stagnant world who aspire to some form of global unity. To these ends, they are prepared to invoke the power of the media and other modern technologies. Unification achieved on the basis of a confrontation between conflicting interests can only serve to widen the gap between rich and poor in the mad rush toward the unknown. Moreover, modern money economies, underpinned by militarist ideologies, dominate the world, trampling underfoot traditional values such as harmonious relationships, generosity, graciousness, and solidarity.

The unity being promoted by the church should not be confused with a utopian uniformity achieved by means of coercion. Instead the church should take the complexity of multilayered social structures seriously, appreciating their deep-rooted cultural and religious origins. To be satisfied with a unity devoid of mutual respect is to be satisfied with unequal relationships in which the stronger exercise power over the weaker. Against the background of these sentiments, the working group noted, "The sacred nature of life and of the dignity of humankind are foundational to the relationships and well-being of peoples."

Specificity of the African Situation

Contemporary Africa comprises more than two thousand population groups (often abusively referred to as tribes or ethnic groups), each with its own language, worldview, spiritual values, and folklore. The colonial experience added another layer of languages, including English, French, Portuguese, Spanish, and Italian.

During the Mombasa Symposium there was much awareness of the current "winds of democratization" that are introducing Africa to a variety of multiparty initiatives. The birth of these parties— often along ethnic or regional lines—has led to the proliferation of groupings devoid of any national, regional, or continental vision.

Added to this cacophony of divisions and conflicts across the continent is an array of religious disputes and an air of competition. It is difficult even to speak of the Christian community as one entity. Christian churches generally are characterized either as "ecumenical" or "evangelical," as if Christians had a choice of being either one or the other! Another major category of African Christians comprises the so-called independent churches, established by African initiative rather than by foreign missionaries. African Christianity is likened to a clay-footed giant, widely recognized and praised for its rapid growth and numerical strength, but vulnerable, meanwhile, to its profound internal weaknesses.

Divisions within African Christianity are rendered even more vexing when it is understood that behind each of the Christian denominations there is support and encouragement from some foreign missionary source. When leaders of such denominations speak of their respective projects, they refer proudly to foreign sponsors. Both Muslim and Christian projects are increasingly dependent on the largesse of overseas support.

The building of community (*koinonia*), transcending denominational peculiarities, should be a high priority for the African church. Only after being brought together around the gospel in a *koinonia* characterized by harmony and solidarity can members of African communities be assisted in building a common future. To the extent that foreigners sponsor individual churches, however praiseworthy the intentions, they may unwittingly undermine the critical element of *koinonia* so important to a credible, harmonious management of diversity in Africa. On a continental level, Africa today may well be witnessing the reinforcement of denominational identities at the expense of rapprochement between Christians of diverse traditions. Entities such as the African Lutheran Association, the Association of Reformed Churches, the Association of Baptists, and the Council of the Anglican Provinces of Africa provide but a few examples.

Role of Christian Councils

According to a paper by Nicole Fischer, presented in absentia at the Mombasa Symposium, Christian councils, whether national, regional, or global, accept difficult responsibilities. They are expected to be the architects of unity in the present, while evaluating the factors hindering its progress and providing the "earnest" or visible expression of a future that is yet to be invented.

Twentieth-century Christian councils are very different from the ecumenical councils that played such important roles in the early church between the years 325 and 787 C.E. They were authoritative decision-making bodies defining consensus for the Christian community with respect to doctrine and ethics, while today's councils function merely as consultative bodies for a still-divided church.

The original intent of today's Christian councils was not to preserve divisions inherited from the past. Some were created as channels for concerted action and as a common testimony by the member churches. Others were created to facilitate more efficient deployment of ideas and resources with a view toward reinforcing the identity and independence of young churches.

Then there is the distinct experience of Zaire, where the government made the decision to recognize Protestants only if they were united under one umbrella. The government-imposed entity known as "Eglise du Christ au Zaire" plays the role of a Christian council. Each member community of the Church of Christ in Zaire retains its denominational status and maintains bilateral relations with its respective overseas partners. The Zairian model is in some respects not the exception; some Christian councils in Africa were imposed by foreign partners or by the larger ecumenical community.

What is important at this stage, however, is neither the initiator of unity nor the number of failures that have been recorded, but our determination to imbue unity with renewed content and fresh objectives.

Generally speaking, Africa's Christian councils have been preoccupied with the provision of joint services and a common testimony through action programs funded almost entirely by overseas partners. Some have been very efficient in the organization of disaster relief services, management of refugee programs, and distribution of funds from outside for church projects. This role has led to the development of astonishing skills in compiling reports and devising project proposals in language pleasing to the donor community. However, the churches have underestimated the contribution that Christian councils could make toward the building of unity.

A deliberate pooling of efforts in proclaiming the liberating gospel is the only one that can lead to the development of a church in which "all of you are one in Christ Jesus" (Gal. 3:28). Collaborative efforts in the preparation of catechisms, in worship, in music, in Bible study, or in the training of church workers would not require any supplementary expenses since each church already carries out all those activities on its own. Cooperation would provide access to the much-needed enrichment from the various traditions.

It must be realized that a unified and loyal church on the African continent will not be built by foreign resources or foreign experts. It will flourish on the basis of the inexhaustible spiritual resources with which God has enriched Africa from time immemorial. These are the resources that African Christians must discover together, submitting them to the service of the gospel, providing the dynamic by which the current crisis can be overcome and the African Christian dream fulfilled.

Communication and Witness

In times past, the "word" in Africa was imbued with the power to heal or to condemn. When the biblical word arrived on the continent, it enjoyed that very same credibility, and its proclamation led to the creation of new, living communities. However, problems appear when these communities, the fruit of the biblical word, face conflicting messages of our modern world, with each message in its own way claiming to lead toward salvation.

As Rev. Chipenda explained in his introductory remarks to the symposium, "In these communities, modern communication is often ineffective because of the distance between the communicator and the relevant public. Communication sometimes destroys individual and collective initiatives, pointing people to illusory realities which cannot be grasped. Our challenge is to create new models of communication in accordance with the cultural and religious heritage of Africa."

Communication that relies for its effectiveness on the sensational will not be able to mobilize individuals and groups to address substantive issues. Professor Mugambi reminded the symposium that oral communication is still very important in Africa today. Many African preachers do not commit their sermons to print, lest they compromise interaction with the community of believers. The fact that many preachers prefer to deliver speeches without referring to written notes at times affects the correct interpretation of Scriptures. Unfortunately, the written word takes on a kind of rigidity, and the shift from the oral to the written word is accomplished at the expense of the human warmth and understanding usually found between an effective speaker and the audience.

Noting that television provides a modest corrective by forging a new link between the message and the communicator, Professor Mugambi warned, however, that "television has fast become such a powerful tool of communication that its control is of major concern both to governments and commercial enterprises."

This new communication medium is presently used to manipulate the message according to the designs and intents of network owners, while the program consumers have become passive receivers of specifically focused messages. Mugambi continued: "Documentation and information management have become so important in the contemporary world that a society which is unable to portray itself according to its own self-understanding will inevitably suffer misrepresentations by others. Africa until the present time has been a victim of disinformation, where the social egos of other cultures have been bloated while that of Africa has been diminished, to the extent that in Europe and North America there is hardly any coverage of Africa in the news. Such news as is reported is always negative, despite the fact that many achievements occur in various countries every day."

Just as Nathaniel was convinced that nothing good could come from Nazareth (John 1:46), so many people think that nothing good can come out of Africa! When Africans absorb these negative attitudes, surrendering their self-confidence, they become subject to manipulation, now believing the negative messages from outside Africa and forfeiting their belief in the power of the "word" to bless and to curse.

Speaking Truth to Power

Just as it was difficult for Isaiah, Jeremiah, and Amos to speak "truth to power," so it is difficult to speak truth to today's political elite. Prophets who dare to speak out against evil may well be risking their lives. Fortunately, each age has its own visionaries who believe in proclaiming the truth at any cost. They identify injustices that destroy the fabric of society and rebuke the powers that be. People in power readily resort to the physical liquidation of their accusers, but they forget the message of African traditional wisdom: "You can throw truth into the fire, but it will never be destroyed." Dr. Menkir Esayas of Ethiopia said, "We still have people on this continent who live under regimes that cannot be fairly judged as free. How does prophetic witness relate to nonfree people in our day and in the future? Do we take up arms to liberate our brothers and sisters? Do we encourage civil war or seek to overturn authoritarian regimes surreptitiously? What would Jesus have said or done for the plight of Africa's voiceless?"

In Africa today, large numbers of people are imprisoned, tortured, or murdered because of their opinions and their convictions. Does not the church's prophetic posture require solidarity with all these victims, whoever they may be? If we do not discern the signs of the times, then our eyes and ears will only be dominated by a communication that serves hidden agendas, a communication not necessarily concerned with life nor the dignity of every creature.

Dr. Esayas described various evangelization campaigns geared to the millennium and asked, "Who tells what to whom, and for what purpose?" Modern communication media constitute a new power bloc. How can questions about freedom, identity, power, and the objectives and consequences of this media onslaught be ignored?

Where can the church stand vis-à-vis an impersonal supracultural power that everywhere imposes its own values, propelling the

world toward unpredictable changes? Will church leaders overcome
the temptation of using the media to keep people ignorant and
infantile, avoiding any discussion likely to disturb the routine operation of church-related institutions? Will Christian communities be
in a position to take advantage of the opportunities offered by the
media for the mission of empowering individuals and groups to face
and resolve their real needs? Can churches set an example of media
use dedicated not to the promotion of mercantile interests, but to
the building of unity among all human beings?

Conclusion

At the threshold of the year 2000, the AACC-sponsored symposium was a unique attempt to shed light on problems and promises
unprecedented and unequaled in the history of humankind. Participants in the symposium had their hope and determination revived,
prepared to imagine a future worthy of human beings created in
the image of God.

But the Mombasa forum was also an occasion to become aware
of the fears that plague African consciousness. These fears are
exploited by sects that make apocalyptic predictions precisely to
attract vulnerable people, detracting from the struggle against oppression. The fear of the future drives some people to live only
for the present, seeking refuge in *anomie,* in alcohol, or under the
glitter of all kinds of illusion peddlers.

The same fear drives African communities to withdraw into tribalism or denominationalism instead of surrendering to unity and to
evangelical ecumenism. This fear, whose seriousness can hardly be
exaggerated, was expressed in Mombasa and discussed in the Bible
studies, the liturgical celebrations, and moments of fellowship.

But God's love destroys fear (1 John 4:18), and the symposium affirmed with utmost certainty that nothing, absolutely nothing, can
separate us from God's love: "neither death, nor life, nor angels,
nor rulers, nor things present, nor things to come, nor powers, nor
height, nor depth, nor anything else in all creation will be able to
separate us from the love of God in Christ Jesus our Lord" (Rom.
8:38-39).

3

Abundant Life in Jesus Christ: The AACC Sixth General Assembly

The Sixth General Assembly of the All Africa Conference of Churches met in October 1992, in Harare, Zimbabwe, under the theme "Abundant Life in Jesus Christ."

More than six hundred persons worshiped together, engaged in Bible study, listened to sobering reports about the state of Africa, and reflected in small groups on a variety of issues.

Participants gathered in sections to focus on four major sub-themes: Vision and Hope, Justice and Peace, Integrity of Creation, and Participation of All God's People. Indeed, discussion on these themes had been happening throughout Africa during the preceding year, and a number of reflections had been published in the AACC bulletin for the assembly, entitled *The Source.*

On the following pages are condensed versions of the reports of each section, written by the Rev. Dr. Setri Nyomi of Ghana, the Rev. Kangudie Ka Mana of Zaire and Senegal, Hellen Wangusa of Uganda, and Edith François of Ghana.

SECTION I: VISION AND HOPE
Setri Nyomi

"Where there is no vision, the people perish." Lack of vision in any organization leads to confusion and inaction. The church in Africa cannot afford to exist without a clear vision, for the lack of one denies its members and our communities the abundant life for which our Lord Jesus Christ came.

A discussion of our vision can be focused by such questions as: Who are we as African Christians? What are we called to be and do in the contexts within which we find ourselves? Out of a sense of clarity of our vision can emerge a sense of hope. This kind of hope

About the AACC

The All Africa Conference of Churches is a fellowship of Christian churches which confesses the Lord Jesus Christ as God and only Saviour according to the Scriptures and therefore seeks to fulfill together a common calling to the glory of one God, Son and Holy Spirit.

It is a Pan-African organ of cooperation and unity for its 136 member churches and National Christian Councils in 38 countries. Headquartered in Nairobi, Kenya, it also has a regional office in Lomé, Togo. The Rev. José Belo Chipenda is the general secretary.

The work of the AACC is carried out in three closely related units:

The General Secretariat (Unit I)
- Office of the General Secretary
- International Affairs
- Finance and Administration
- Information, Library, and Documentation

Selfhood of the Church (Unit II)
- Youth and Women
- Theology and Interfaith Dialogue
- Christian Education and Family Life

Service and Witness (Unit III)
- Research and Development
- Refugee and Emergency Services
- Communication Training Centre
- ACIS/SIEA

The AACC's president for the past five years, Desmond Tutu, the Anglican archbishop of Southern Africa, was re-elected at the 1992 Assembly for another term. The four vice presidents, elected to represent the other major regions of the continent, are:

West Africa: The Rt. Rev. Kwesi A. Dickson
East Africa: Mrs. Mary Auma Owuor-Jalang'o
Central Africa: Mme. Rose Zoe Obianga
North Africa: Bishop Serapion

The General Committee, chaired by Bishop Tutu, has twenty-three members representing West, East, Central, North, and Southern Africa. An equal number of alternates is elected at each Assembly.

Since 1963, the AACC has held a General Assembly on an average of every five years. The themes have been as follows:

Kampala 1963	Freedom and unity in Christ
Abidjan 1969	Working with Christ in Africa today
Lusaka 1974	Living no longer for ourselves but for Christ
Nairobi 1981	Following the light of Christ (John 21:15–19)
Lomé 1987	You shall be my witnesses (Acts 1:8)
Harare 1992	Abundant life in Jesus Christ (John 10:10)

is rooted in current realities and our response to God. It is not to be confused with optimism or wishful thinking. We can grasp our vision and hope only when we look at our identity in relation to our role within our communities.

As the church in Africa, we are called by God's name; we have responded to the good shepherd who brings in life in its fullness. The question is: Are we or our communities experiencing this abundant life? A look at the daily realities in which people live and the critical issues that face us on the continent make it very difficult to give a ready affirmative answer to these questions.

Critical Issues Facing Africa Today

Africa is confronted with geographical, human, ecological, economic, and spiritual factors that require analysis and action. The following are just a few:

1. The effects of slavery and colonization are still with us. Very often with independence, only the color and nationality of the oppressor changed. At the same time, the colonial powers continue to exercise control.

2. Many countries are struggling to be freed from dictatorships and one-party systems of government. Meanwhile, the dictators are clinging to power, resulting in human losses. For many countries, this attraction to multiparty systems comes with very little clarity in meaning.

3. Double standards are exhibited by our governments in their utterances and actions.

4. Ethnic clashes and civil wars abound.

5. Militarization affects all, especially young persons.

6. Problems in many countries often lead to disruptions in education. Universities are closed down for extended periods.

7. Lack of economic resources often make us vulnerable to conditions dictated from outside this continent.

8. Dependency on external resources leads to various programs being drawn for us from outside our continent.

9. The debt crisis is growing.

10. Mismanagement by governments is seen too often.

11. We have unreliable economic bases to depend on for economic growth.

12. There is an information gap between grassroots and experts on economic strategies.

13. The church is often unsure of its identity, often leading to a decision to hide under a semblance of spirituality that is blind to the destruction and injustice going on around us, or a decision to abandon a meaningful spirituality relevant to and inclusive of all (young and old,

women and men, lay and clergy). This leads to the church being seen
as without a vision and passive.

14. The church inadequately addresses issues touching on social jus-
    tice and peace and is not a real prophetic voice in this era of
    multipartyism and the demand for democracy.

15. The church's processes of decision-making are often very undemo-
    cratic. When the churches themselves do not understand what de-
    mocracy is, how can they be a prophetic voice to undemocratic
    governments?

16. Religious multiplicity and pluralism challenge the church in two
    ways. With the spread of Islam and its influence, sometimes the
    church is in the minority, is itself marginalized, and finds it difficult
    to act. There is need for dialogue.

17. The churches lack boldness and courage. They often have a need to
    be liked by the governments, and so they would rather wine and dine
    with the governments than be prophetic.

18. The churches lack unity.

These situations place stress on the people, families, and communities of Africa. The close-knit families that characterize much of
Africa seem to be giving way; the disintegration of both extended
and nuclear families has grave consequences for children.

The Leadership Crisis

There is a need for a quality of leadership in all spheres of life that
will inspire hope and help deal with the issues outlined here. Alas!
Africa has a leadership crisis in church and society.

The leaders often focus on their own need to stay in power and
therefore often exclude voices of challenge. They see themselves
as ends in themselves and go to any lengths to ensure they are entrenched in office. Leadership is often removed from the reality of
the people and has not cultivated the ability to listen to people before formulating policies. Such leadership is unable to use the skills
and knowledge represented in pockets of the community clearly
felt to be a threat, such as women, youth, and persons of different
opinions.

This situation is just as prevalent in the churches. An example is
the feeling of indispensability. African leaders just do not know how
to leave office and make way for others whom God may choose.
They cling to power.

Church leaders often see themselves as uncritical allies of oppressive governments, often baptizing their programs. That our
churches are afraid to be a challenge in our communities shows a

The Big Man

In addressing the Mombosa Symposium in 1991 on the sociological effects of religious movements, theologian Paul Gifford sketched an image of the "big man" as he appears in Africa under single-party rule: "The big man's face is on the money. His photograph hangs in every office in his realm. His ministers wear gold pins with tiny photographs of him on the lapels of their tailored pin-striped suits. He names streets, football stadiums, hospitals, and universities after himself. He carries a silver-inlaid ivory mace or an ornately carved walking stick or a fly whisk or a chiefly stool. He insists on being called 'doctor' or 'conqueror' or 'teacher' or 'the big elephant' or 'the number one peasant' or 'the wise old man' or 'the national miracle' or 'the most popular leader in the world.' His every pronouncement is reported on the front page. He sleeps with the wives and daughters of powerful men in his government. He shuffles ministers without warning, paralyzing policy decisions as he undercuts pretenders to his throne. He scapegoats minorities to shore up popular support. He bans all political parties except the one he controls. He rigs elections. He emasculates the courts, he cows the press. He stifles academia. He goes to church."

This somewhat caricaturized description contains elements of truth. Many African countries have been led by despotic leaders who controlled the state apparatus without any participation by the people. Gifford states, "Big men, in their attempt to secure total personal power, have in many places coopted the mainline churches. The mainline churches have thus effectively become part of the structures of dominance....In many countries big men with dubious commitment to accountability or human rights hold important offices in mainline churches. Often churches have allowed themselves to be bought by favors and privileges, and they fête and honor the big man on whom they depend. Of course there is nothing particularly African about this."

misunderstanding of the biblical mandate. The Bible is read in a way that misses its message calling us to fullness of life in all its aspects.

Our churches are not united. Denominational lines and divisions among ourselves are so entrenched that we are usually unable to pull our resources together and act together against the forces of evil. Given the existing structures, the voices that are able to respond to some issues are often excluded because of their gender, age, or creed. Moreover, there is an educational gap. The church is not investing enough in young persons who are able to lead in responding to the issues. Those who are trained are often unable to use their knowledge and skills because they are perceived as threats to the establishment.

So long as these problems are found in the churches and we are not responding to the issues that affect us, we have compromised the credibility of the church. We proclaim abundant life but live in communities that are asking: Where is it?

Sources of Hope

Can we then ever talk of abundant life in this world? On this continent? A critical reading of the Bible rooted in a critical analysis of these issues leads us to an affirmative answer, which constitutes our hope.

The essence of the gospel is the story of God's emptying of self to identify with humanity, wearing the title of the suffering servant and dying on our behalf to overcome sin and all forms of evil. The gospel is both the self-emptying and the glorious resurrection. The hope that this inspires, therefore, includes the certain knowledge of God's understanding of and identification with human suffering.

Unlike wishful thinking, it does not pride itself mainly in looking forward to another era when unpleasant situations will be no more and we shall all live happily ever after. Hope recognizes that even now, in the middle of the struggle, God is with us. As Jesus Christ concluded in the great commission, "I will be with you always." God is on the side of the suffering and those who are called to proclaim the good news to them (Matt. 28:16f).

God's promise to sustain life and to prosper the endeavors of the faithful (Isa. 65:19–25) is not merely a call to look forward to material prosperity as a reward of faith. It is a reminder of the radical interest of God in doing something about the hopelessness in society. Another prophet saw this as God's ability to bring even dry bones to life (Ezek. 37). A biblically based conception of hope is one always rooted in God's action and human reality.

Although we are still overwhelmed by our struggles, we can see signs of hope. Many young persons and students have demonstrated courage and boldness in speaking out, standing for, and sometimes dying for the voiceless on critical issues. Though isolated and not commonplace, there are prophetic voices. Sometimes these voices prophesy with great opposition from their own churches. Although many countries are experiencing birth pangs, democratization and transitions to multiparty systems are going on in some countries.

The AACC has responded often to issues that affect the lives of communities on the continent, and some Christian councils in some circumstances have responded as well.

While we celebrate these signs of hope, we must be aware that abundant life does not just fall from outer space onto our laps. A concrete analysis of the issues and our biblical mandates should lead to concrete actions.

A Call to Action

In Ezekiel's encounter with God in the valley of dry bones, Ezekiel was not merely a passive spectator as God turned the lifeless dry bones into living beings. He was God's instrument. After affirming that the bones could come to life, the Lord said to Ezekiel, "You prophesy to them." Our hope that the helplessness, hopelessness, and brokenness we see around us are under the judgment of God and therefore cannot be allowed to wield power over us can become a reality when we hear God's voice saying, "You prophesy to them." We are called into action as instruments of God, not compromising with the forces of death but being prophets, bringing good news to the suffering and to the voiceless, bringing abundant life into lifelessness.

God's message of hope always includes responsibility for the people of God: "If my people who are called by my name humble themselves, and turn from their wicked ways, . . . [I] will forgive their sin and heal their land" (2 Chron. 7:14). In view of these messages, we recommend the following actions:

If we want our land healed and abundant life realized, then we have to repent. We have to repent where there is apathy in the church. We have to repent for having exclusive structures often worse than the structures in the secular society. We have to repent of our selfishness and tendency to cling to power. We have to repent of our lack of accountability. We have to repent of our inability to listen to our own people. We have to repent of our running away from our prophetic roles like Jonah. We have to repent as individuals, as churches, as denominations, as national councils, as a continent-wide conference of churches, as leaders and members.

After repentance we can work hand in hand with God in bringing about a more just society, acting concretely within the church and in relation to society.

Within the church, we must:

1. Turn back to the Bible and be ready to fulfill its mandates.
2. Be serious with our stewardship; see our responsibility to use our time, talent, and possessions (tithes, etc.) for God's work within church and community, and not merely wait for these resources to be brought to us as passive recipients.
3. Effectively include young persons in every aspect of the life of the church. This means:
    - training young people and giving them the opportunity to take up leadership positions in the church;
    - utilizing the knowledge and skills of young persons already trained in the church;
    - establishing youth desks in churches and national councils that do not have them and strengthening those that do;
    - staffing these youth desks with actual young people in accordance with AACC guidelines, with sufficient resources for their operations;
    - establishing intergenerational committees to seek ways of ensuring cordiality between young persons and church leaders and ensuring that the young are not in turn the new source of oppression for the old.
4. Find new meaningful ways of doing things that are done traditionally in the churches:
    - have a workable program of exposing people to the good news of God's liberation in Jesus Christ—liberation from sin and from the forces of death and oppression destroying us in our communities;
    - encourage Bible studies that challenge us, leading us to analyze current realities in ways that challenge our apathy and empower us to lay claim on the fullness of life;
    - provide meaningful counseling services to support persons and families dealing with issues that confront them; provide meaningful pastoral care;
    - be prophetic in messages from the pulpits.
5. Listen to people instead of coming to people as briefcase-wielding experts. We need to create an open community.
6. Look within our own churches for human and material resources, first and foremost, instead of to Europe and North America.

In terms of society:

1. The church should stop being silent. We need to be the voice of the silent.
2. Churches should attend to the needs of children in our communities as a priority. We should develop our own programs and also support programs of other organizations, such as UNICEF. We should include a program for street children in programs of the AACC youth department, associate member national councils, and member churches.

3. The AACC and national councils should take up the issue of dealing with the foreign debt crisis, advocating reduction or elimination.

The AACC and its member churches should engage in some general actions as well:

1. Do serious work in research and planning and develop literature related to the issues that confront us.
2. Cut down on internal expenses, so that we can increase expenditures on action responses to the issues that confront us in our communities.
3. Base our actions on a critical analysis of ourselves. For example, do the resources we spend on programs and our statements of concern about the drought and other problems reflect our commitment when compared with how much is being spent on the structures within which we are having this assembly and the food we are eating here?
4. Recognize what is being done by other nongovernmental organizations in order to avoid duplication and also to work cooperatively.
5. Take the lead in advocating for the marginalized of all kinds.
6. Program for theological education to reach as wide a circle as possible through extension programs.
7. Facilitate information flow at all levels.
8. Encourage education that trains people to use hands and skills. Church policy-makers should make funds available to support the development of talents and skills. This will be a contribution toward dealing with unemployment.

In all these, the church in Africa should be united and speak with one voice.

SECTION II: JUSTICE AND PEACE
Kangudie Ka Mana

The Rev. Frank Adubra led the group with a passionate and lucid communication describing the context of Africa today as "this jungle of injustices," from which we have to come out to build the "new Jerusalem."

Our continent has been stifled and strangled by many an injustice, ranging from our poverty-stricken peasants to the despair of unemployment in the towns, from constant famine to the catastrophe of AIDS, from the disasters of one-party dictatorships to the most murderous civil wars.

Justice is the condition for peace in the most concrete acceptance of the term: personal integrity, material well-being, happiness, peaceful coexistence, an end to conflict, a state of equilibrium, harmonious relations; adherence to consensual politics that integrate the interests of all (including minorities); organizing the privilege of discussions, negotiations, dialoguing, and solutions.

Out of this vision of injustice and peace, the church's role is clearly defined:

- not a church that stoops to compromise and complicity with dictatorial and bloodthirsty powers, but a church that is resolutely involved in the fight to come out of the jungle of injustices;
- not a church of fine words or beautiful principles based on a tame or euphoric reading of the gospel, but a church where the good news is a real liberation of all those who are oppressed by the powers of injustice and conflict;
- not a church in retreat from the fundamental challenges of society, but a church that has strength in its proposals, its solutions, and its construction of the "new city of Africa."

Carried on the winds of liberation and reconstruction, this church can only work for the birth of democracy in Africa, "a New City with men and women capable of acting for radical transformation, through breaking the chains of inequality, high-handedness, and divisions," thus establishing and expanding the reign of abundant life. This is the task of the church in Africa—to build up a new way of thinking, to expand the ethics of liberation and reconstruction, and to structure the whole African being on the whole of life.

Our group reflected on strategies for action by African church communities and by Christians in our countries in their struggle for justice and peace.

1. We recommended that a Pan-African Committee for Justice and Peace be established. Integrated into the present framework of the AACC's Department of International Relations, this committee would:

   - organize facilitating activities, training, and education for justice and peace in the churches of Africa. This would mean setting up a network of reflection and action by ordinary church members as well as national and continental structures for a liberating reading of the Word of God.
   - intervene in all the pressing situations that demand that the church speak out, protest, and be involved in a process of reconciliation. It would mean relying on honest church people who have credibility and the ability to be politically minded.

2. We recommended that training, education, and conscientization programs in churches and ecclesial movements be implemented to meet the problems of justice and peace. A whole bundle of proposals emerged from our discussion:

- setting up a training program for Christians on the framework of an overall project in specific centers, such as Mindolo, Zambia, for Anglophones and Porto Novo, Benin, for Francophones;
- developing a pastoral approach to the family and a program for participative education for greater awareness of the questions of justice and peace;
- actively involving the churches in government programs of education for citizenship;
- organizing the political formation of pastors and lay preachers as well as promoting a "holistic" teaching to understand the whole range of society's problems; to see questions of justice and peace as essential dimensions of Christian faith in its incarnation in the heart of specific social contexts;
- identifying civic institutions that deal with human rights with a view to working in an articulate way with the churches responsible for justice and peace.

All these strategies would be meaningless if they were not seen as church strategies in the context of mission in today's world. The General Assembly was asked to consider them in this light and to entrust the Pan-African Committee for Justice and Peace to carry them out in concrete fashion.

3. On the question of democracy, we were against the myth of the glamorous democracy of a race or culture. We strongly affirmed that democracy is a universal value that implies both the participation of people in decisions that concern them and a creativity for all, so that power will never be confiscated by an individual or a party. Democracy as such is not an end in itself but the instrument of social well-being and the flowering of individuals. It is not an "open, sesame" for a people lacking ambition but a conquest and a claim to be permanently defended by all living forces. To carry out these essentials for democracy, we should:

- involve young people in mobilization campaigns;
- form groups in the church for reflection; and
- form continent-wide networks for training and action.

SECTION III: INTEGRITY OF CREATION
Hellen Wangusa

"Go into all the world and proclaim the good news to the whole creation." So says the Risen Lord in his farewell discourse to his disciples at the end of Mark's Gospel (Mark 16:15). Salvation is not only for us human beings, but also for the whole world, indeed for all creation. It is in Christ that "all things hold together" (Col. 1:17), for in him a new heaven and a new earth (Rev. 21:1), a new beginning for us all, has already started to come into being.

Our preaching must therefore proclaim this new creation; our actions must show it forth and our churches must be at the forefront of the struggle to save the earth and fill it with God's goodness.

For God it was who made the world and all that is in it, and God made it very good (Gen. 1:31). So, too, the Holy Spirit is rousing all our churches, across the continent, to work together for the regeneration of our African environment. It is the Spirit, the One given to recall to us all things (John 14:25-26), who is reminding us at this hour that we are to be co-creators with Christ.

In order to give birth to that abundant life that Our Lord holds out to us, we must cooperate with God and with all our fellow creatures to restore the world to its original splendor. We must learn to sing God's praises together with all the good things that God made, for God made them not only for us, but for themselves and for God's own greater glory. We must cease to be the destroyers and exploiters of the creation and become instead its stewards and preservers.

When Jesus called himself the good shepherd, he pointed out how different he was from the thief and the brigand who come only to "steal and kill and destroy" (John 10:10). The abundant life he promises comes from the earth that sustains us. The salvation he brings is the restoration of the proper relationship between all God's creatures.

Whatever disrupts this relationship has its origins not in the good shepherd, but in the thief. Christ commands us to oppose, firmly and clearly, whatever destroys the environment that God made out of love and that God entrusts to us for our well-being and its safe-keeping. We must prevent the kind of destruction that needlessly kills off animals and plants, and even our fellow human beings, through lust for power and greed. We must oppose whatever turns our African earth into an uninhabitable desert, for when this happens we are stealing from our children and our grandchildren a resource and a heritage that is theirs by right and that is our duty to pass on to them.

Our recommendations are by no means comprehensive. We nevertheless hope they will inspire the churches of Africa to take the theology of creation seriously and rouse them to safeguard, sustain, and nurture the particular environment in which they live and serve.

> ## *The Care of the Ancestor Spirits*
> In some traditional African societies, the chiefs, who are viewed as custodians of morality and justice, are buried in sacred caves, whence their souls are believed to protect all forms of creation from abuse. It is said that people who kill more animals or pick more fruit than they need for food, who fell more trees than they need for fire-wood, who use abusive language or utter derogatory remarks about other forms of creation in the forests suffer from temporary disori-entation and lose their way back home. This is said to be the male elder ancestor spirits' warning for offenders to respect the right of other forms of creation to exist.
>
> Female elder ancestor spirits are said to be the nurturing spirits who lead weary and hungry travelers in the wilderness to water, food, and honey, sometimes guided by the honey bird.
>
> *—Jane Mutambirwa*

Problems and Their Causes

Deforestation is a major issue. People cut trees to prepare fields for cultivation, to get firewood for cooking, to use the lumber for building their homes or to sell commercially. In Kenya there is con-troversy about the destruction of coastal forests for the building of beach hotels for tourists.

Where nomads are restricted to small areas or where the num-bers of cattle or goats per acre have increased, overgrazing and the destruction of grass results. The quality of the soil degenerates be-cause exposed soil is easily washed away in the rains or blown away in the dry weather. This is aggravated by open-strip mining or by the accumulation of dumps around underground mines.

Droughts that periodically ravage parts of Africa are aggravated by deforestation and soil degradation. A story came from Kenya of a well that had served the community reliably for many generations. When it suddenly ran dry, the people traced the problem to the felling of a very large tree nearby. After some years, shoots grew from the stump of the tree and gradually water came back into the well. This illustrates the interaction of trees and water supplies.

Farmers and gardeners have been encouraged to use chemical fertilizers and pesticides without consideration of the effects of these chemicals on the environment. For example, pesticides have resulted in birds producing eggs with very fragile shells.

World economic pressures have had a devastating effect on the wild animal population of Africa. For example, the rhinoceros used to be widespread in Africa, but it is now a critically endangered species because poachers have been killing rhinos to get their horns for sale to Yemen (for dagger handles) and China (for medicine).

Air and water pollution follow the establishment of industries and the growth of large cities. Many large companies are far less concerned about preserving the quality of the air and the water than they would be if they were in Europe or North America.

Vast urban migration has created great slum areas, which often have problems with sewage disposal, poor water supplies, and rapid spread of disease. Urbanization also has contributed to the disintegration of the traditional extended family. For example, in traditional society an aunt or other village women would be responsible for teaching girls about their sexuality. Such relatives are not readily available in an urban setting.

Modern society produces large amounts of waste products, such as plastics and metals, which create major disposal problems in cities. Cows can die as a result of eating a plastic bag, and yet these things litter the countryside.

African communities have become dependent on the sale of primary products to developed countries. Many of these commodities have lost value in real terms while the equipment needed to produce and process them has become more expensive. There is an increasing and worrying dependence on Western technology such as hybrid seeds and a fear that African products will be produced in Europe while African countries get poorer and poorer.

The prevalent attitude of greed and the frantic struggle for more possessions and more power is in direct contrast to the tenth commandment, "Thou shalt not covet." Even Christians have become infected by the attitude of grasping more possessions and power. This is in direct disobedience to God's call to a simple lifestyle, in community with others rather than in competition with them.

Strategies for Action

In southern Sudan, seminomadic people depend on cattle; they give medicine to their cattle before themselves because the cow means marriage, sacrifice, and food. In the same region, the chief decides the number and size of the fish to be caught, to avoid overfishing and the killing of young fish.

In Ethiopia, the church and monasteries made a tradition of planting trees around their premises. Some of these trees are two thousand years old. Cutting them is forbidden.

Some communities in Uganda and other African countries at one time kept rivers, streams, and wells sacred, and no one could dare violate the water. The whole community cleaned the wells regularly. A clean and well-tended farm was the pride of the community, and the crops were planted with the animals and birds in mind. Out of respect for the forest and the big trees, the community allowed hunting or collecting only what was needed by the family.

In Nigeria and many other countries, tree-planting days are established to rehabilitate the rain forest that has been destroyed. Communities must maintain and care for the new trees until they are well established.

The churches must voice the importance of environmental issues, pointing out their theological and ethical significance and encouraging positive programs of action to deal with them. The following recommendations were made:

1. Every member church of the AACC, including their training centers and theological colleges, should appoint an advisor on environmental issues. This person should be responsible for research at the local level and for organizing programs to inspire people to action. Areas to be looked into are biological farming, horticulture, forestry, fuel conservation, charcoal-making, organic farming, slash-and-burn or shifting cultivation, drought resistant crops, and nomadism.

2. Churches should organize tree planting programs and give annual reports on their progress to the AACC. Cutting trees without replacing them should be seen as a sin against God and creation, a failure to fulfill our duties of stewardship.

3. Every local congregation should have a small tree-nursery program. In fact, each should acquire land, plant trees, and declare that holy land. All Christians should be made to care for their own immediate environment; homes and churches should be a good example. One Sunday a year should be set aside as "Creation Sunday"; creation should be the theme for the sermon.

4. Women, being the most intimate with the land and young people, should be allowed to participate in raising consciousness about environmental issues. The community should be educated through programs of youths, women, and children, and through the mass media.

5. Patience should be inculcated into Christians to safeguard against the current drive for instant results.

6. The church should reactivate the biblical notion of rest every seven years or find new expressions for that concept. Africa needs the rest that goes with repentance if the environment is to be redeemed.

7. The church must change from promoting the theology of salvation over and above that of creation.

8. The churches should promote the renewal of African religiosity and cultural understanding of life and creation.

9. The clergy and the laity need to be educated to appreciate creation. Creation theology and all its practical implications must be introduced into the curriculum of all theological colleges.

10. Churches and the AACC must denounce governments or multinational corporations whose programs are destructive of creation.

11. People should be encouraged to write useful and practical literature that promotes good methods of farming, soil use, and the general preservation of all God's creation.

12. Funds allowing, training of trainers should be organized.

SECTION IV: PARTICIPATION OF ALL GOD'S PEOPLE
Edith François

The speaker for this subtheme, Brigalia Bam of South Africa, gave credit for the courage the AACC had shown in risking the choice of the theme "Abundant Life in Jesus Christ," when in Africa one would rather speak of abundant violence and death, mass starvation, displacement of millions, drought, AIDS, and marginalization. She observed that "participation of all God's people" has always been on the agenda of the ecumenical movement since its inception. The terminology and emphasis may change, but the problem remains the same.

The current crisis involving Africa is not only economic, legal, political, and social. Tragically, it is also the nonparticipation of the vastly impoverished majority in socioeconomic and political development, which stems from an overcentralization of power. The individual and collective creativity of women, youth, and peasants is severely undervalued, underutilized, and even curtailed. The church is not an exception to such guilt.

On the other hand, governments are losing ground in their influence over the lives of the people. In an era of openness and growing people's movements, fear of tyranny is slowly disappearing. The culture of tolerance and democracy is growing. As nations cannot be built without the support and involvement of all the citizens, who are their greatest resources, the people therefore must be empowered to determine their priorities. Imposition of ideas and structures on people in development usually fails. Participation is the driving force for collective commitment to decisions that affect people's lives at all levels and at all times.

Jesus, in his ministry, did not focus on people with religious and political power but announced the kingdom of God to people who were marginalized. Our speaker focused mainly on women and youth as those unduly marginalized. She observed that the church in Africa has been influenced by society in its attitude toward women and its silence on issues that dehumanize women in society is of great concern. The church should shake off lethargy and traditional beliefs, customs and cultural practices that are obstacles to women and undermine the status of women in church and society. However, they should recognize and value those beliefs and practices that contribute to development.

The church should also strengthen women's capacity as builders of confidence, encouraging rural and urban organizations to initiate and implement strategies for participation.

Youth should be supported in their efforts to organize national autonomous associations to enhance their full participation in all activities and programs of society. Impediments such as bans on their associations, police brutality, detention, and harassment, as well as frequent and arbitrary closure of educational institutions should be eliminated.

Some key conditions for ensuring people's participation in Africa are:

1. Cessation of all wars and conflicts. The resources spent on defense should be redirected to useful activities and social services. This will better the situation of refugees and displaced persons who have no opportunity to participate in the planning of their own future.
2. Equitable distribution of income and other material resources to all.
3. Promotion of mass literacy. The church should mobilize the many skills available to it for services in the community and training, because participation is possible only if people have the skills, confidence, and spiritual strength to participate.

After Mrs. Bam presented her paper, the floor was opened for discussion. I must say that the time allotted for discussion did not give the chance to each one of more than a hundred of God's people gathered at the "Participation" subtheme section to participate fully! Nonetheless, many issues were raised.

The group strongly noted that participation is a God-given fundamental right for all God's people, so it is not a side issue. Moreover, as the issue of participation has been discussed several times, it is now important to act. Some issues were related particularly to young people or women, others to marginalizing situations.

The Youth

The Constitution of the AACC ensures the participation of youth. However, very often the young people, like the women, are relegated to physical chores and excluded from decision-making or policy formulation. They are not to be implementers only.

Young people would like to sit together with elders to discuss all matters affecting the church and its structure. That is the only practical education they can get. Elders should not be threatened by the fact that if they help the youth to stand up and walk as Peter and John did for the cripple, the youth might begin to jump and do the unexpected. The youth should be challenged and guided to what they would like to do.

However, the church should be wary of manipulated participation of the youth. In some countries, young people are seduced into taking arms because of rampant unemployment; they get paid by those who arm them to participate. If the church could tackle youth unemployment by encouraging and creating projects for youth, their active participation would not cause bloodshed but would enhance life.

Other hindrances were identified. Young people are victims of drug and sex abuse in Africa. They cannot participate in anything but rather are liabilities to the societies in which they live. The church is urged to wage a campaign against drug abuse and teenage parenthood and the AACC encouraged to devise a strategy for "birth planning."

One problem cited is that the AACC operates only in the capital cities, and communication to the villages is virtually nonexistent. Also projects for youth and children are very slow in taking off (if ever there were any).

Women

Women should be encouraged and given the chance to train, to get confidence and exposure to ideas they are not aware of, e.g., ordination of women.

Participation by representation is inadequate. There should be the sharing of tasks through delegation and flexibility in structures to allow for changes in the church and governments.

Unfortunately, the problem of women's marginalization partly stems from socialization processes adopted by women themselves for their children. Consequently, women fail to support each other; for example, in elections they pull each other down.

An interesting observation was made that not only women and youth but also men are marginalized. There are youth and women's desks but no men's desks. Women form the majority of most church congregations. The question is, Where are the men?

Interfaith Relationships

One poignant area of concern discussed at length was interfaith relationships. God's people include all humankind. In many parts of Africa, there is conflict between Christians and Muslims. Delegates gave testimonies of the atrocities carried out against Christians in some countries. Muslims are going all out with proselytization to the extent of enticing people with money and other material goods or intimidating them. Muslims also are gaining power over governments. Some strategies proposed to foster cordial interfaith relations are:

- to pray unceasingly for the spirit of God to guide and lead the church;
- to educate people on peaceful coexistence so they do not exclude other faiths who join the worship;
- to encourage holistic community project planning that includes all faiths;
- to create a large seminar or other forum where representatives from countries grossly affected by the interfaith conflict may be invited to discuss and tackle the problem. Dialogue on interfaith relations should be done cautiously, with mutual understanding and respect for each other's faiths.

Development

The church is urged to intensify its education so that people can participate in the formulation of criteria for development projects. Whenever an international agency is invited to a country for project planning, the church should know about it to give input.

The church should not only react to government policies but should be involved in all the decision-making processes. For example, the church should be represented in local parliaments, the AACC should have representation in the Organization of African Unity, and the World Council of Churches should be represented at the UN.

Democracy and rights are new concepts in Africa, and in its educational activities the church should be wary of democratization that results in legalizing despotic leaders. That is, popular participation must not mislead people to create something worse.

The church is asked to define its type of education. Will it be an informative or empowering education? A liberating or domesticating form of education? The church must decide at which level it should intensify its education, bearing in mind that in many countries educational institutional programs at the higher level are arbitrarily interrupted. The church is advised to train trainers, beginning with a crop of faithful, committed groups who understand what they are doing, to enable them to penetrate the society.

People should be taught how to be committed to a cause. Seminary training should be revised to upgrade the graduates on the direction of the church as a consequence of conferences such as this. In fact, the clergy and church leaders should begin implementing recommendations from conferences such as this!

Power should not be overcentralized, giving room for unnecessary speculation about corruption and nepotism in the church. The church should focus more on people than its clergy, to uplift the society at large and render services to all, with integrated development and without discrimination.

The churches should remember that "oral illiteracy" is one potent hindrance to effective participation. Even if a person cannot read and write, that person has some mental acumen that can be harnessed through oral participation. The AACC experienced oral nonparticipation at the Assembly because Portuguese and Spanish were absent as working languages.

In order not to marginalize the clergy, we all need to act as one people, God's people, learning to worship as a unified group. We should minimize divisions in church denominations. We should integrate city and rural folk for development and seriously consider the church's stand against other faiths. Our action will begin from the individual's own attitude toward participation. The more we take off our masks, the more transparent we become to see and respect each other's dignity. We can place ourselves in each other's shoes to understand each other and to enhance effective participation.

4

Women's Perspectives

ABUNDANT LIFE FOR WOMEN AND CHILDREN?
Edna Maluma

Our Lord said, "I came that they may have life, and have it abundantly" (John 10:10). What does abundant life mean for an African woman? Representative answers to this question include:

- "To have the basic necessities of life, like food, clothes, and shelter. If I am in possession of these, I am at peace with myself and the Lord Jesus Christ."
- "I should be able to send my children to school."
- "Abundant life for me means affordable health care."
- "Abundant life is not necessarily money, though that too is essential. Do unto others as you would like to be treated."
- "It refers to happiness, to acquire what you need, the freedom to do what you want without any restrictions."

Preventing realization of the abundant life are numerous mechanisms of oppression that have an especially negative impact on women.

The Mechanisms of Oppression

One of the most important factors in determining access to any level of employment is **education**. A vital link exists between access to education and the potential for self-sufficiency. Information is power, while ignorance was and still is a factor in the subservience of women. Equal access to education or training of all types at all levels for girls will enable them to develop their personalities and participate equally with men, thus achieving self-reliance, family well-being, and improved quality of life. Due to economic crises sweeping the continent, the majority of Africa's illiterate people are women.

The gap between boys and girls that was beginning to narrow between 1950 and 1980 will be wider now, because more and more

---

This essay is a condensation of the presentation by Edna Maluma of Zaire to the Committee on Selfhood of the Church at the AACC Assembly in Zimbabwe in 1992.

families are being driven into poverty. With limited finances, families continue to give boys preference for education. Even after entering school, girls tend to abandon school for reasons such as pregnancy and to do household chores.

Throughout Africa, there are many women who work sixteen-hour days. Though vital to the functioning and productive activities of any society, women's **work** remains unrecognized and is given little or no economic value. In terms of paid labor, women are plagued with low pay and low-status jobs and consequently suffer more from impoverishment. Certain jobs traditionally have been designated as either for males or for females. Time and again women are deemed unable, unreliable, emotional, and incompetent. Women are on the receiving end of social prejudice, including sexual harassment, at places of work.

Social bias also can be noted in agriculture. United Nations statistics show that 60 to 80 percent of subsistence food in Africa is produced by women. But women usually have no access to credit facilities with which to improve their production. It is not surprising, therefore, that African countries are suffering from chronic hunger. New technologies meant to reduce workloads go to men, while women continue utilizing burdensome implements for farming. Very few women receive training in agriculture; male extension officers generally pass information on to fellow men.

For a rural woman, the hours of work are extended because of the need to walk long distances for water and firewood. According to UN statistics, the world's women perform two-thirds of the work but receive only a meager one-tenth of the income and own only one one-hundredth of the property. Women are the poorest of the poor due to unjust economic policies. Is this the "abundant life" promised to African women?

Reductions in public spending for **health care** affect women more than men. Care of the sick and elderly falls squarely on women. When rural health centers close down for lack of drugs or personnel, women suffer the effects. When a malnourished child is admitted to the hospital, it is the woman who spends cold nights at the child's bedside and in the mother's shelter. Due to stress and inadequate quality food, some women experience miscarriages and premature births.

Peace is not only the absence of war, but the absence of exploitation, oppression, and disregard for human rights and dignity. **Violence** against women takes the form of domestic violence, rape, incest, sexual assault, and harassment. Such violence cuts across class, religion, race, and geographic boundaries. It is devastating to be beaten and molested by someone who is supposed to be demonstrating love and care. The home, which is intended as a place of safety, has become a dangerous place for women. Young girls are forced into sexual relations to secure jobs in the current harsh economic environment. In the process, some have contracted HIV.

According to the World Health Organization, the majority of Third World women suffer from iron deficiency anemia. Inadequate intake of protein, coupled with constant childbearing and rearing, adversely affects African women's health.

Some **cultural practices** in Africa constitute hindrances to women's realization of abundant life. For example, tradition dictates that a man is offered the best food and is expected to eat first, with children receiving second priority, and the woman invariably last. In times of food scarcity, women must make do with less nutritious and less appetizing leftover foods or are expected to eat a different diet altogether.

The death of her husband brings added misery for a woman in some African tribes. She is made to feel guilty for the death, is mistreated, stripped of property, and left to fend for herself and her children.

The Struggle for Survival

A large proportion of households in both cities and towns, as well as rural areas, are headed by females. Women are engaged in all sorts of survival activities. They sell food and other goods in the market and in the byways, come rain or shine, cold or heat. Even married women engage in such business, as some husbands are unemployed. Still other women have taken to illegal gold panning. Some are engaged in sexual work fraught with the danger of sexual diseases. Others have taken to stone crushing, sometimes losing fingers in the process. Women who deal in cross-border trade learn to cheat and bribe in order to get their merchandise through border entry points.

The destruction of the created order has an impact on women. As they are responsible for supplying water and fuelwood for their families, deforestation and drought mean that women have to trek further and further to find these necessities. Insufficient water also leads to poor hygiene and unsanitary conditions, which in turn are the source of diseases.

Amina

Amina is an Ethiopian now living in Somalia. It is dawn after the previous night's downpour of rain. She searches in the darkness of her tent for a few sticks of more or less dry firewood. These few sticks are all that remain of the two-day supply for which she had walked for six miles. On the way back she was stopped and beaten by the local people who robbed her of most of the wood. Accepting the pain and fear, she resumed her journey with what was left of the precious fuel. Then she carefully put it on the earthen floor of her tent to prepare a small meal for herself and the three children who were sleeping on the cold damp floor.

Only two months ago, she and her husband were together in their small home 100 kilometers away in the south of Ethiopia. The fields and the animals which supported their modest living are just memories now, things of the past like her husband and eldest son. After walking for six hours toward the Somalia border, they and fellow travelers encountered an armed patrol. Her husband and son were shot in the ensuing confusion.

Now Amina is alone to fend for herself and her children in an unfamiliar and often threatening environment. Camp officials shout and wave their sticks at her while she waits for food rations. Strangers from other lands move through the tents each day, asking questions that she does not comprehend. Her youngest son is sick with a body rash, but she is not sure which of these strangers should be asked for assistance. Perhaps today she can take the child to the corrugated iron building where her neighbor was given medicine. At any rate, she will first have to stand and wait her turn at the water supply. And then there is the problem of getting more firewood, necessitating another long journey. This time she will be more careful. (Thompson, Refugees UNHCR, June 1986, p. 3)

Amina's story conveys a deep sense of human tragedy and misery experienced by female refugees. They encounter other problems, more than male refugees, including excessive domestic duties, sexual coercion and abuse, general discrimination, and illiteracy.

According to the United Nations High Commissioner for Refugees, the majority of refugees worldwide are women and girls. Refugees are the product of forces that are all too familiar to most of us: the apartheid system in South Africa, the colonial legacy, civil strife and cross-border warfare, tyrannical leadership, and natural disasters.

Starting life afresh with few possessions in a foreign country where one may be unwelcome is difficult. One may be unable to communicate with people or unable to find means of survival. A refugee is poorly sheltered and fed and could well die of illness or hunger. Thousands of refugees have died from all sorts of difficulties. Traumas faced by refugees include the painful decision of leaving one's homeland, job, friends, and family members, acquiring a sense of rootlessness, and witnessing death and violence against loved ones in the course of flight.

Child Survival and Development

Happy children can be observed on a daily basis, and that is good. But not all children are smiling. Some are victims of child abuse and neglect. Child abuse may be physical, sexual, or emotional, or it may take the form of general neglect, the failure to provide such necessities of life as warmth, food, attention, supervision, and normal living experiences.

In most African societies the family is a very important social group. It is in the family where needs such as care, food, shelter, and feelings of belonging and love are met. But economic readjustment programs, implemented at the expense of social services, threaten the well-being of the already poor, who are bound to bring up another poor generation. Children are being asked to repay the debt with their malnourished bodies, weak brains, and, for some, their lives.

Unfamiliar urban settings and industrialization, resulting in the breakdown of the extended family system, also threaten child survival and development. Generally, movement from rural to urban centers triggers child neglect. The proportion of families in which a woman is struggling to rear her children without a mate is larger among migrant families. Out of work, some men desert their families.

Large families, ignorance of nutritional needs, inadequate community water supplies, and poor sanitation all contribute to poor child survival and development. In rural areas, a child's well-being may be at stake because family farms are small and infertile. In the name of development, multinational corporations in conjunction with governments have taken land from the poor for export cash crops to pay off debts.

Because the home environment is unfriendly, poor, and neglected, parents may divorce and separate, and the children run away from home in search of a better life. These children are a familiar sight to all of us. They roam the streets of cities and towns all day long, dirty and dressed in tattered clothes. They experience violence and police harassment. They are arrested for loitering and suffer abuse, scorn, and neglect while they struggle to make a living on the streets. They go hungry for long periods and lack shelter and adequate clothing. They are involved in a wide variety of activities, including guarding and washing vehicles, selling all sorts of goods, and carrying heavy loads like bags of mealie-meal for payment.

Since children make up nearly half of the total population in developing countries, the satisfaction of their needs should be our major concern. The church should be courageous in taking deliberate and effective measures ensuring the well-being of our children and freeing them from persistent subhuman conditions. It is not enough to baptize a child; there must also be an expressed concern for survival and development.

Challenge to the Churches

Women's participation in the church is still under dispute. For a woman to win a top position is a struggle. Lay women continue to be minimally represented among denominational decision-makers. Like any male counterpart, women may sense a call into the ministry of God and Jesus Christ. That women are called to be God's messengers, prophets, and disciples is clear throughout the Old and New Testaments. But because official church prayers speak of God, Jesus, and the Holy Spirit as masculine, there is always the assumption that women are excluded from such ministry.

At the conclusion of the UN Decade for Women (1975–85), zero change was noted in women's participation in decision-making and leadership positions. In the world of today, many types of oppression persist. These include racial discrimination, economic exploitation, violation of human rights, and political domination. But when patterns of sexist oppression are cited, even the most enlightened people shake their heads in embarrassment, smile helplessly, or assume an air of arrogant disapproval.

In most churches today women constitute a majority and function as the main contributors to the maintenance of churches, while in matters of decision-making they remain the most marginalized. The church should be the last to practice sexism but, unfortunately, it is in the forefront.

WHEN WOMEN RISE THE EARTH TREMBLES
Musimbi Kanyoro

I once caught my grandmother using a proverb she had just used the day before in a different context. I objected, pointing out that the two occasions were contradictory. She sat me down and gave me a lecture, explaining that proverbs are sayings that are pregnant with meaning. The context of the proverb determines its meaning. Proverbs are like shadows. You have to move with them and they have to move with you.

When I consider the situation and actions of women globally, I draw from my grandmother's wisdom the power for survival. The massive evidence of our lives as women shows that in many cases our strong voices are being heard merely as whispers. We do so much, yet so little improvement seems to be reflected in our status. We still carry the image of poverty, despite our contributions to the economies of our countries. We advocate peace, yet we live in perpetual fear of violence inflicted on us. We can go on with this litany of sadness, but that is not what my grandmother's wisdom taught me.

Our lives are like proverbs. The context defines the meaning. We have to celebrate and name women's strength and determination to refuse marginalization of any kind. We must resist the labeling of women as victims. Rather we must work to empower women by affirming their actions and enabling their voices not to be silenced. Yes, it may seem in some cases as if women's strong voices are being heard merely as whispers, but in many other cases, those same voices cause the earth to tremble.

Lifting the Skirt

Kuoerwo muthuru is a saying in the gikuyu language that literally means "lifting the skirt on someone." It refers to the worst curse that a mother (or any older woman) can inflict on her adult child (or any younger person) in utter disgust. (In this African context every woman is a mother to everyone who would qualify to be her child.) For an older woman, mother or grandmother, to "lift her skirt" is to publicly declare that she has tried every possible way to communicate to the child, but instead the child despises her to the point of

This essay is condensed from a speech presented by Dr. Musimbi Kanyoro at a conference on "A Female Perspective on the Year of Jubilee" in Sigtuna, Sweden, in May 1993. Used by permission.

disregarding the fact that she is the mother. The act literally says, if you don't believe my motherhood, let me show you the path from which you traveled. A woman uses this gesture only as the very last resort after exhausting every other channel of resolving the dispute.

This is what the mothers of the political detainees did in Nairobi's freedom square in 1992. The women were on a nonviolent hunger strike demanding the release of their sons and news about their well-being. They sat at a small corner near the Anglican cathedral, singing hymns and holding placards stating their grievances. They attracted attention and sympathy from crowds. The authorities realized that these powerless old women who were virtually unknown were gaining power as the press began to cover their story and expose details of their grievances. The police attacked them. They threw tear gas at the women. The crowds were angered and retaliated by hurling stones and bottles at the police. The police continued their attack insisting that the women must stop the hunger strike. The women refused to stop.

In anger, amazement, and disgust at the police attack on them, the women lifted their skirts. With this ultimate rejection of intimidation, they registered their scorn for the actions of the police. They were stating that no one can rob them of the power of womanhood, the power of birthing through which they experience the pain, the concern for life that they bring forth. It is this determination of women to resist that causes the earth to tremble.

Women's Movements

We have all become familiar with the legendary Mothers of the Plaza de Mayo in Argentina demanding news about their disappeared children. The example of their silent demonstration has spread to all parts of the world. In Israel the "women in black" (mainly Israelis) stand in vigils throughout Israel every Friday from 1:00 to 2:00 p.m. to protest the occupation and the resultant violence. The women dress in black to symbolize the tragedy for both the Israelis and the Palestinians. They hold signs calling for an end to the occupation. They withstand the insults from hot-heads as well as from their own family members who do not hold their views. Women-in-black movements have sprung up in other countries.

Women's actions of resistance have brought the issues of rape, sexual abuse, and other forms of violence to the attention of the public. The UN commission on the status of women has taken violence against women as one of the issues on which to lobby governments. Because women spoke up about Bosnia and other situations, rape was put on the agenda of the human rights world conference in Vienna in June 1993. In other instances, indigenous women and those women living under racism have more than proved to the world the double oppression resulting from domination and cultural enslavement. We are all aware of the struggles of women like Winnie Mandela of South Africa, Wangari Mathaai, the Kenyan environmentalist, and Rigoberta Menchú, the Guatemalan Nobel peace prize winner. Their stories are not individual stories but real struggles of women the world over.

Women act to support life. Women's movements are creating one of the far-reaching social revolutions of our time. At the international level this revolution can no longer be ignored. At the Earth Summit in Rio de Janeiro an unprecedented number of women's organizations participated. Concrete recommendations on how to increase attention to women and their perspectives on issues is woven throughout Agenda 21, considered the major achievement of the Rio conference.

Whenever issues of justice have been addressed it has simply been thought that women automatically would benefit from any good that resulted to the society in general. The trickle-down model currently under heavy criticism in development circles is, however, not being sufficiently challenged on issues of gender discrimination. Wholesale assumptions for women are not in order. Constitutions and laws of the countries of the world, for instance, stipulate that all people are equal before the law. But in practice this equality for many women exists only on paper. In my country a woman still needs the consent of her husband to obtain a passport even if they are no longer together. The same law does not apply where the man presents the request. The first issue for any Jubilee, in the biblical sense of the term (see Lev. 25), is to address the status of women.

What would the Jubilee do for the sad faces of the children, women, and men that I met in the refugee camps in Malawi? I remember the story a young girl of fourteen years told me. Her family was murdered in her presence, and she was hit and left for dead. Somehow she was rescued from among the dead and survived after several months of hospitalization. At the refugee camp, she has no one to trust. The older women almost enslave her, expecting her to perform all their difficult tasks like fetching water and collecting firewood. The frustrated idle men see her as a tool to meet their sexual needs. She is frightened to sleep or to be alone, yet there is no one to hear her out and attend to her special needs. In tears, she asked, "Why did I not die with my family?"

Jubilee and Empowerment

There is no possibility for a Jubilee for women unless we make the links between what happens to women today and the concepts that the biblical Jubilee stood for. Slaves were to be set free. What about the contemporary forms of slavery? Women's lack of personal freedom is an enslavement. Women's unvalued and unquantified labor in the home is slavery. Violence in society aimed at women is a form of slavery. Think of sexual trafficking of women, rape, physical beatings in the home, the burning of brides, involuntary circumcision, denial of land ownership rights or rights to education, to shelter, to water, to health, to food, and for some the right to vote.

Values that are either hostile to women or do not take women into account need to be addressed. Issues of women's status and those of national liberation, independence, social justice, democracy, and so on have to be seen as related. Resistance against foreign powers — be they colonial governments, multinationals, the IMF, the World Bank, aid agencies, or church structures — cannot be separated from the struggle that the women are mounting as they advocate their own freedom. A country cannot be liberated if half of its inhabitants are exploited by culture, class, patriarchal values, or gender biases. If a Jubilee would not give at least 50 percent of the freed resources for the benefit and use of the women, it would not be Jubilee at all.

What do we need to do then? We need continued dialogue between men and women, for in a way we are all enslaved. This is not an issue of men against women, but rather a world built on wrong premises that have now been standardized over the ages. For me this is where the Christian faith is a great help. As a Christian, I am allowed to begin again. I am allowed to admit failure, and I know that if I change direction, my past is not held against me. What I need most is the strength and courage and humility to admit that things are not right and I can try again with the help of God.

The solidarity that women advocate is that which recognizes that injustice has to be done away with for all. It has to be "Justice" not "just us." The limitation of people to their clans is not a concept that we can subscribe to, even if we extend the symbol to nations as we know them today. My own country, Kenya, is experiencing a lot of pain right now due to the so-called clan ownership of land.

The practice of particular groups feeling that they and only they have this or that right is tearing our whole world apart. Whether it is tribalism and apartheid in Africa, nationalism and racism in Europe, castism in Asia, or Zionism in the Middle East, it is still the problem of "we" and "they." We, the very special, entitled, chosen people. Unless the resources available can be used for everybody who is in need, the justice in Jubilee is questionable.

If you pick up a newspaper in any part of the world, you are likely to find a story about women protesting some injustice. Women's grassroots movements and professional groups, as well as individual women, have played their roles in creating pressure and influence. Women are presenting new alternatives that affect traditional thought systems. Governments, schools, churches, courts, and homes are all being challenged. Women's movements are about the future of the church and the future of society.

MISSION STATEMENT
FROM THE AACC WOMEN'S DESK
Omega Bula

The Women's Desk came into existence in its present form immediately after the Fifth General Assembly of the AACC in Lomé, Togo, in 1987. From its inception, the Desk has worked to mobilize women for effective participation in church and society. With the declaration of the Ecumenical Decade: Churches in Solidarity with Women (1988-98), the mandate of the Desk was broadened.

The work of the Women's Desk has been hampered by the relative weakness of the collaborating intermediary organizations, a majority of whom fail to discharge their facilitating roles. The heavy dependence on external funding and the backdrop of structural rigidities within ecumenical structures have also presented problems. On the other hand, the Desk has been inspired by the readiness of women to participate in all programs, by the exemplary work of some of the intermediaries and Desk staff, and by the continued support received from our ecumenical partners.

Over the last four years the Women's Desk activities have been implemented by means of workshops, seminars, study groups, lead-

Omega Bula of Zambia is the program officer of the Women's Desk of the AACC. This is a condensation of a mission statement written by a gathering of women and men in Nyeri, Kenya, in June 1993. Used by permission of the AACC.

Domestic Dissatisfaction

Women often say their problems are not with their family roles and functions but with interpersonal relationships in the home. They cite:

- lack of communication, appreciation, and respect by their partners and extended family about their roles and function;
- lack of communication on fertility, birth spacing, and number of children the couple's finances can support;
- lack of communication on how to manage the couple's finances. In one study women said they did not mind how poorly paid their husbands were, but that their husbands did not discuss financial problems with them.
- being blamed for the wrong sex of the baby. In African tradition male children are often preferred to females because they pass on the seed.

—Jane Mutambirwa

---

ership development skills, and production of resource materials relevant to the work of church women. The emphasis has shifted from the traditional missionary women's work of prayer, song, service, and charity to programs that address life issues.

Our Biblical Mandate

The work of the Women's Desk is based on Christ's mission, "I came that they may have life, and have it abundantly" (John 10:10). The mission is perceived as participation in the healing of all aspects of life: spiritual, physical, social, economic, cultural, and political. This healing mission embraces individuals, communities, and the environment through its programs on economic justice, child survival, health, and food security at the household level.

The Women's Desk has always looked to the life and mission of Jesus as a model of openness, empowerment, inclusiveness, challenge, and affirmation.

There is an acute awareness that the crises tearing at the heart of Africa have their most pronounced effect on women, even as they struggle against all odds, bearing their burdens with great fortitude. The Desk is committed to the creation of an enabling environment, empowering women to triumph over human-made crises in an effort to heal the entire community of God's people. The search for abundant life, justice, and sustainable development proceeds through the restoration of women to full participation in community with men, youth, and children. There cannot be economic justice in isolation from political justice.

The Women's Desk likens its participation in the healing mission to the mission of Mary, mother of Jesus. From the time the vision is announced, through its articulation, acceptance, and realization, Mary remains a partner with God and bears this vision in community with others despite the political, economic, social, and cultural difficulties of the day. This demonstrates the preparedness to recognize a vision and accept the commitment it entails. Inspired by the example of Mary's mission, we undertake the following initiatives:

- helping men to understand that the struggle is a communal effort, not to be carried out by women alone; that in Christ we are one body and "if one member suffers then the whole body suffers";
- launching unconventional initiatives because God acts through us; we are chosen, we are on a mission to renew the old, to bring new vision and hope;
- mobilizing power despite powerlessness and vulnerability, in solidarity with other women in the struggle; our liberation is bound up with that of others;
- recognizing the signs of solidarity between men and women based on our common struggle for survival and development;
- ensuring creativity in problem-solving, in overcoming passivity and hopelessness;
- questioning the status quo; no condition need be permanent.

Our Focus

The Women's Desk is aware that its vision and mandate calls for work on a wide front and with a large number of issues. However, in view of limited resources and in view of the interrelatedness of the issues, it has been determined during the next five years to focus on the following:

1. The Economic Strangulation of Africa

In spite of abundant God-given resources, human-made factors have brought the continent to the brink of economic collapse. The imposition of IMF–World Bank Structural Adjustment Programs, commodity prices, a ruthless free market, and the debt burden have together dissipated Africa's resources. This scenario has also led to the ever-rising cost of living, the falling prices of raw materials, the overexploitation of natural resources, an increasing gap between the rich and the poor, cuts in social services (health, education), rising unemployment, unacceptably high mortality and morbidity especially of children and women, AIDS, the breakdown of family units and community support systems, and comprehensive abuse and violence (cultural, social, economic, gender, and spiritual) especially of women. Therefore we affirm our work on economic justice, literacy, and awareness-building, enabling women to effectively address issues that affect them, their families, and their communities.

2. Democratization of Africa

In our effort to heal broken communities and achieve solidarity, we must confront undemocratic power systems that prevent God's people from participation in formulating both the religious and secular domains. This implies working to eradicate inequitable power distribution, lack of accountability and transparency, systematic violation of human rights, near total exclusion of the majority (both women and young women) in decision-making and advocacy, rigid power structures in the church, as well as division and disunity within the church and across denominations. We affirm our work in the promotion of popular participation to empower individual women to effective work in church and society.

3. Community and Household Support

We intend to focus on:

1. Mobilization for churches' participation in community-based health programs.
2. Child survival as an integral part of the healing of broken communities and a guarantee of a healthy future for the church and society.
3. Food security at the household level as a foundation for the struggles of women for community sustenance and eradication of anxieties.
4. Exchange programs and study visits for mutual self-empowerment of women.

The Desk operates principally as a facilitator and enabler. Ours is a fully participatory approach at all points of the partnership circle, linking the Desk with national Christian councils, member churches at the continental level, as well as with the World Council of Churches and all other ecumenical organizations.

5

The Challenges of Governance

CHURCH AND STATE
IN AFRICAN PERSPECTIVE
Tokunboh Adeyemo

Africans live in a religious world. Unlike their Western counterparts, Africans perceive, analyze, and interpret reality through their religious grid. In 1979, Britain experienced excessive snow. The prime minister, James Callaghan, appointed a minister of snow to handle the situation. In the same year, Kenya experienced a severe drought. The president of the nation, Daniel arap Moi, called a day of national prayer and went to church on that day. In these examples one sees in sharp focus the contrast between a mechanistic worldview (Western) and a mystical worldview (African).

Africans in general (black Africans in particular) believe that the visible, tangible, and material world is influenced, and even controlled by forces of the spirit-world. The world as a natural order that inexorably goes on its ordained way according to a master plan or, worse still, is left to the mercies of human beings and science is foreign to the African mind. The African believes that the invisible world of the spirits (including the ancestors) has a lot to do with the visible world. Consequently, those who have access to the invisible world and are believed to be able to manipulate the spirit-forces (such as religious leaders, witch doctors, and juju/medicine men) are not only respected and venerated in the society but also feared. Take, for example, the Ogbonis, a strong and powerful secret cult of the earth among the Yoruba of western Nigeria. The Ogbonis are revered and dreaded, and it is commonly believed among the Yoruba that nearly every great Yoruba statesman of yesteryear was a member of this cult.

In this type of system, the following socioeconomic and political implications are worth noting:

Dr. Tokunboh Adeyemo of Nigeria is the general secretary of the Association of Evangelicals of Africa and Madagascar (AEAM). Printed in the booklet *Africa at a Crossroad,* this speech was delivered at the TEAR Fund (U.K.) East Africa Conference at Limuru, Kenya, on February 20, 1991. Used by permission of the AEAM.

71

1. Leadership in the traditional society was acquired by possessing mystical (or magical) power or military might, or by inheritance, or by being wealthy and generous, or a combination of these. Appointment to public office was by selection rather than election and the process was secret.

2. Positions and powers were usually retained for life unless one fell out of favor with the ancestors.

3. Governments in traditional society had no opposition party as in modern democracy. Those opposed to the powers-that-be were treated as rebels.

4. Blood line running through extended family, clan, and tribe was very strong. The corollary to this includes nepotism and tribal favoritism.

5. Moral values were preserved by religious taboos rather than through parliamentary legislation.

6. A ritual attachment to land, especially one's ancestral home, made mobility in pursuit of economic development difficult.

7. A mystical explanation of events sometimes bordered on fatalism; the need for shrewd, strategic planning was sacrificed at the altar of bad or good luck.

8. No firm distinction was made between religious and political life, between church and state, so to speak.

9. Religion and religious personages occupied a place of pre-eminence in traditional society. Instances abound where religious kings have been deified.

10. Traditional religion survived long after the demise of traditional states (due to colonization) and in diaspora (e.g., in the Caribbean and the Americas).

Church and State during the Colonial Era

The history of slave trade and subsequent colonization together with the invasion of the continent by Islam and Christianity has affected the culture of African peoples to a large extent. Islam, like the traditional African worldview, does not dichotomize sacred and secular. Islam means submission and peace and requires Allah's rule over all of life.

The position of the church in Africa during the imperial era was ambivalent. On the one hand, "civilization and Christianization" were allied (an identification model); on the other hand, the emerging self-governments and indigenous/daughter churches were kept as two distinct entities (a separation model). Part of the reason for this was the deference to Islamic religion by colonial powers. Writing on the church in Nigeria, Andrew Walls states that the colonial government did much to protect and promote Islam and Islamic institutions, especially in the northern part of the country. While individual Christians were not forbidden from running for a public office (they were the best trained), the state preferred to have the mission/church at a distance, under the claim of running a secular government. According to Pastor Mutava Musyimi, this approach "served to minimize direct interference with her activities and made control easier. . . . The end result was a mission (or church) that was largely collaborative, dependent, and vulnerable."

But there was yet another model of relationship to emerge during this period. With the rise of nationalism and the struggle for independence in the 1940s and 1950s, the church by and large played the role of a protagonist of the African cause. While the church would not participate in oath-taking as in the Mao Mao (there were exceptions of course), it was nevertheless as committed to the liberation of its people and land as the freedom fighters. Most of the pioneers of liberation movements were products of mission schools. They refused to accept the alienation of the church from public and civil matters by the state. Nationalist Joshua Nkomo spoke for many when he said: "Africans must look to their ancestral spirits for inspiration in the national struggle."

As recently as 1985, Canaan Banana, then president of Zimbabwe, castigating a separatist model, said, "Christianity holds an effervescent and vibrant recipe for social transformation. We believe that Jesus came to save the world, but in which way? How can it be possible that He came to cleanse the soul of each individual from sin without being concerned about the social consequences of injustice and exploitation?"

Not all of the church has been "separatist" all of the time. One recalls with gratitude the role of such men as William Wilberforce, David Livingstone, Lord Shaftesbury, and Martin Luther King, Jr. Their heroic example of standing for justice and speaking for the voiceless is a transformational model of meaningful engagement.

Church and State after Independence

With power changing hands in the 1960s the move of the new elite was toward centralization, consolidation, and silencing of critics. The one-party state became the order of the day, or military juntas were in power. Ironically, the church, which by and large fought alongside the nationalists for independence, was being pushed to the sidelines. In some instances its role as partner of the state in development was recognized; in some, its institutions (such as schools and hospitals) were nationalized. Almost invariably, the church was marginalized in power-sharing and at best given a ceremonial role of reading prayer at state functions.

The church found itself struggling for survival and pushed either to support or oppose the regimes. More often than not the church capitulated and supported the political status quo. The evangelical churches have been more culpable in this regard. Occasionally the church stood with the poor and the oppressed and spoke with prophetic power, but this often has meant persecution of the leadership of the church, as in the case of Archbishop Janani Luwum of the Anglican Church of Uganda, who suffered martyrdom under the reign of Idi Amin.

Without any let-up in discharging its evangelistic and missiological mandate, the church (particularly evangelical) is more and more aggressively taking a stand in the marketplace. Issues of national and international interest are being addressed by individual denominations and national evangelical fellowships. New fora of dialogue and cooperation are being forged. The Rev. Joseph Imakando, general secretary of the Evangelical Fellowship of Zambia, told of a joint delegation of his fellowship, the Christian Council, and the Catholic Secretariat to the State House, making a common presentation on behalf of the church in Zambia. Similarly, the Christian Association of Nigeria, a body representing nearly all ecclesiastical traditions and diverse theological positions in Nigeria, has not only written and spoken with one voice on national issues but has organized protest marches on such matters as citizens' rights and justice.

In November 1990 a historic conference was held at Rustenburg, South Africa. Attended by 230 participants from 80 different denominations (including the Dutch Reformed, the Roman Catholic, member churches of the SACC (South Africa Council of Churches), member churches of the Evangelical Fellowship, and independent churches), the week-long conference focused its worship and deliberations on the theme "Towards a United Christian Witness in a New South Africa." A declaration was produced and presented to the state president, Frederick De Klerk.

A new phenomenon of publicly combining priestly, prophetic, and evangelistic roles, of combining separation with cautious identification, of crossing traditional ecclesiastical boundaries, and of running for public office as a Christian with church backing is what I describe as a new wave of church and state relationship in Africa.

Where does it all lead? It may be too soon to predict. Contributing to a seminar on political ethics in 1989, Dr. Odunaike remarked that "a secular state is not the same thing as an irreligious state. . . . The separation of church and state should not mean that Nigeria as a nation should be a nation free of religious influence."

Both church and state are divine institutions with distinct, separate, but not altogether unrelated roles to play. They should complement one another. A doctrine of total separation as advocated by Martin Luther is alien to the African worldview. The position of the Roman Catholic and Orthodox churches, of the church above the state, approximates the traditional African view more closely. However, given the historical and cultural changes and the doctrinal development of the subject in the New Testament, an "alliance posture," such as that of the Church of England or John Calvin's doctrine of both under God's law, seems more appropriate. Never must the church deify the state (as in Zaire), nor become so identified with it (as the Dutch Reformed Church in South Africa before its confession in 1990) that God's higher claims are compromised. The church must maintain its cutting edge: not of this world, yet in this world.

THE CHURCH AND DEMOCRATIC TRANSITION IN AFRICA
José Belo Chipenda

In Africa nearly all countries are abandoning one-party dictatorial regimes and seeking to move toward more pluralist political structures. They are striving to define and identify themselves with the term "democracy." We in the All Africa Conference of Churches have followed closely these recent developments. What is not yet clear is whether the new wind of change blowing all over the continent is divinely inspired or again humanly engineered, as it was with the 1884 Partition of Africa and in 1954, when the International Monetary Fund and World Bank were launched.

The church in Africa, being people-oriented, is participating in the ongoing democratic process at different levels. In some countries, such as Angola, Kenya, and Mozambique, it produced material to educate people for democracy. In others, such as Benin, Mozambique, South Africa, Togo, Zambia, Madagascar, and Namibia, it

This is an edited version of an address delivered by the Rev. José Belo Chipenda of Angola, general secretary of the AACC, delivered in December 1991 at the AACC Partners meeting in Washington, D.C., and used by permission.

facilitated the democratic process through mediation. In still others, such as Rwanda and Burundi, it facilitated the relationships between the two main ethnic groups, the Hutu and the Tutsi. Almost everywhere, church participation in African democracy is best realized when Roman Catholics and Protestant churches work together.

Democracy, as it is viewed in Africa today with its many definitions, has emerged with different shades, based on differing expectations. The accepted definition is "rule by the majority, but ensuring protection of minority rights." Some think that democracy is a natural result of the collapse of socialism in Eastern Europe while others say that it is a tool for the creation of a New World Order. There are people who wrongly identify democracy with political multipartyism or with free-market economics.

Oketch Owiti, a lecturer at the University of Nairobi, has said that "as Africans seek to explore new methods of democracy, there are questions that need to be clearly addressed and, if possible, answered. For example, What exactly is democracy? Can democracy exist where poverty, economic and social injustice, political inequality, and power abuse exist? Can democracy exist where the ideas of right and wrong are confused?" We could also add, Can democracy exist where people are dying of AIDS and people cannot pay school fees for their children? The World Health Organization estimates that at least nine million African children under the age of ten will lose one or both parents due to AIDS by the year 2000. Until these and other questions are answered, we will continue to play with words with unclear meanings.

Let us examine for a moment a number of events that shed light on how Africa is being moved to accept democracy.

Professor Adebayo Adedeji pointed out in Arusha in February 1990 that in Africa, "three decades after independence, our people continue to be excluded from critical and significant contribution to the ethics of the body politic. Basic rights, including individual freedom and democratic participation by the masses, are increasingly absent from Africa."

In March 1990, Archbishop Desmond Tutu preached at the All Saints Cathedral in Nairobi, Kenya. Fully aware that militarism breeds violence and corruption, he told the audience that "freedom is cheaper than repression." Later on, Giovanni de Michelis, Italy's foreign minister, suggested that countries cutting their military budgets should be rewarded with increased access to aid and loans.

Going further, he said that developed countries should commit a larger proportion of their GNP to development aid.

In April 1990, Smith Hempstone, U.S. ambassador to Kenya, delivered a speech in which he warned that in the future the United States would give preference in economic aid to those nations that nourish democratic institutions, defend human rights, and practice multiparty politics.

In June 1990, the Organization of African Unity launched the African Charter for Popular Participation in Addis-Ababa, Ethiopia. Soon afterward, the president of France, François Mitterand noted, "Without democracy there will be no development in Africa."

In May 1991, the Africa Leadership Forum held in Kampala, Uganda, identified democracy, political pluralism, strict observance of human rights, good governance, public accountability, popular participation, sound economic management, and genuine cooperation as decisive signposts for the future.

A Second Liberation?

Within the context of the current so-called Second Liberation of Africa, the first outburst of democracy was manifested in Benin and now proceeds unabated across Africa.

Examples of the growing pains of democracy are numerous. In Gabon, the main opposition leader was found dead in a hotel room in Libreville; in Ghana, multipartyism created a sensation among the population. In Kenya, the government complained that the Church of the Province of Kenya (Anglican) was too active in politics; in Ethiopia the university was closed to silence the voice of students; in Luanda, Angola, there was a blackout that lasted for weeks.

From September 1990 to October 1991 ten heads of state in Africa were voted out, toppled, exiled, or murdered. During the same period, Francophone countries held their national conferences, presided over by the clergy, while heads of state, until then revered, were suddenly confronted with people's power. Presidents Mobutu of Zaire, Eyadama of Togo, Denis Sassou Nguesso of Congo, and Habyarimana of Rwanda were publicly humiliated and their private lives exposed.

The Anglophone countries changed their constitutions and embarked on the long road toward elections. Angola and Mozambique, as well as Ethiopia, Guinea, and Guinea-Bissau, dropped their adherence to Marxism and legalized opposition political parties.

Today multiparty politics is legal in forty-one of sub-Saharan Africa's forty-seven nations. In 1992 alone, multiparty elections were held in at least eighteen African nations. Only Sudan and Equatorial Guinea maintain their authoritarian regimes untouched.

Crucial Role for the Churches

The role African churches played in the democratic process has been crucial. The church, Protestant and Roman Catholic alike, has produced trustworthy leaders for these critical moments. When the credibility of politicians waned, trust was transferred to heads of churches. This was seen in Benin, beginning in February 1990, and in Togo, since 1991. In Cameroon, Mozambique, and South Africa, churches have played important catalytic roles.

Through public statements, denunciation of violation of human rights, pastoral letters, visits, representations to governments, publications, and workshops on peace and reconciliation, churches have greatly contributed to the current change in Africa. Church documents usually start with an affirmation of the churches' responsibility to stand for the truth; they continue by describing concrete, living situations and the need for repentance.

The work of the AACC at this juncture has been that of facilitator. It began in 1988 and has continued until now. Countries that have been assisted include Angola, Burundi, Cameroon, Ethiopia, Liberia, Madagascar, Mozambique, Rwanda, and Togo. What has been learned is that:

- assistance to liberation movements was much easier than trying to help people involved in the ongoing democratic process;
- Protestant churches are well equipped to denounce evils in society but are less able to suggest viable options when needed.
- changes witnessed in most countries are of persons and not of quality in leadership;
- democracy in Africa raises more problems than it solves.

The naive belief that a combination of democracy and multipartyism will bring prosperity is false. Countries that have gone democratic in the last few years are not doing well economically.

With democracy we see the emergence of new sources of conflict. Whenever political leaders invite people of the same tribe to join them, there is a problem. The same problem arises when outsiders, trying to influence and control the future of a given country, financially support recognized political parties as points of entry.

For this reason we say: While democracy is good in principle, we should not lose sight of the dangers multipartyism can introduce into the African body politic. An inflated number of parties does not make a country democratic; instead, it is the freedom to accept without discrimination the best contributions coming from free citizens that makes a country democratically progressive.

In this regard, we see the role of the church as crucial in the coming years. The church should not conform to the values sanctioned by the present transitory society. It should instead participate in championing what is new and lasting.

Church leaders participating in the democratic process in Africa should embark on the development of valid options for the future. On the one hand, there are loud cries of people with acute human needs to be met. On the other hand, the church knows that men and women do not live by bread alone. They need the bread of life that Christ alone can give. We are at the point of intersection between the human and the divine. On the one hand, we need to discern what God offers humanity, and on the other we need to discern new ways of helping human beings grasp the presence of the divine in their daily lives. It is here where work and worship meet, where proclamation of the gospel and social action converge, where true religion and honest politics find common ground. We are convinced that abundant life in Jesus Christ is possible only when those who are freed from the constraints that used to oppress them accept to share in words and deeds with those who do not know Christ.

WHEN THE WRETCHED OF THE EARTH SPEAK!
Musimbi Kanyoro

The governors of Africa do not take politely to different opinions, let alone criticism. Their reactions are often so intimidating that people are forced to consider whether the course they are advocating is worth their life and that of all their dependents. For when punishment is dished out, the associates of the victim are not only left unprovided for but they also become suspect.

This essay is condensed from a paper presented at a workshop on Communication and Prophecy sponsored by the World Association of Christian Communication, Africa Region, and EDICESA (Ecumenical Documentation and Information Centre) in Lusaka, Zambia, late in 1992. It appeared in a similar format in the WCC publication *One World* in June 1993. Used by permission of the author.

In November 1992, a BBC news bulletin gave the public a good illustration of the extent of fear that exists for the governors of our nations. The BBC yielded to pressure from the British Council not to run a production of *Macbeth* filmed in Malawi by the Shakespeare traveling theater. It was argued that Malawi's president had been too closely associated with Macbeth. It was feared that President Kamuzu Banda would be so enraged that he would vent his rage on the local staff who had helped the Shakespeare group to give the interpretation to this play!

The ailments of Africa are often closely linked to the governance of the continent, although the issues are by no means solely internal. The area of economic development has been one of the disappointments of Africa. During the first years of independence, many African countries experienced capital flight from wary investors who feared that Africans would unleash vengeance once they took over the reigns of power. Then came the era of foreign aid in form of loans, grants, or both. Loans were either soft or hard; grants were either in the form of commodity aid, capital and technical assistance, or military assistance. Unfortunately, this foreign aid did not deliver the hoped-for economic development. In fact it has ended up retarding it. Today most countries can hardly pay the interest on the loans, let alone pay off the principal. Caught up in the debt trap, social services, health facilities, educational institutions, food, water, and shelter facilities have collapsed, exposing the populace to misery and death.

One regime after another, promising to be the panacea to the situation, have but used it for their own benefit. African leaders have failed miserably to mobilize, organize, direct, and control the resources and personnel of the continent toward the attainment of meaningful self-governance. Instead the leaders' greed and thirst for power coupled with a strong dose of short-sightedness have caused them to build a fortress around themselves by investing in a small selected group whom they empower to be a buffer between them and the masses. This group of collaborators together with the leadership receive huge dividends in terms of unlimited access to wealth and privileges, which they in turn dish out to their relatives and friends, thus forming another ring around the leadership.

Whether external or internal, Africa's impediments are self-reinforcing and self-perpetuating, and it is not a wonder that today we can boast of excelling in internal wars, starvation, and illnesses of every type! We also can boast of well-defined and functioning systems of corruption and mismanagement of resources. Against this background, the majority of the people of Africa, especially the children, the youth, the women, and all categories of the poor in the rural areas and the urban slums, can only be described as "the wretched of the earth."

Can "the wretched of the earth" speak out? Can they speak for themselves? Can their voices be heard beyond the dark cells in which they are imprisoned by hunger, illness, illiteracy, poverty, wars, repression, and charity? Does popular participation in communication have a chance to reach the ears of those who govern nations, let alone influence their decisions?

Popular Participation

It does not take literacy for people to feel hungry and to beg for food. However, it takes a special type of formative education for individuals and communities to ask, "Why are we hungry?" and "What can we do to get out of this situation of want and need?" Begging addresses the immediate need, while asking the deeper questions seeks to delve into the root causes and the sustainable improvement of the situation. The first approach addresses an immediate need that can be curbed quickly and easily by importing food or by responses from the international community. The second approach is foremost an internal issue, and it can destabilize the governance of nations if it is pursued to its logical end. The first approach allows room for pity and the consequent charity, while the second requires accountability based on responsible management with inherent checks and balances so that the "whys" and "hows" become joint responsibilities of all the citizens.

Governments, agencies, and even religious groups easily respond to immediate needs for which results can be quantified, but recoil in horror or benign amusement or embarrassment at the prospect of a quality education that equips people to know how to ask their own questions! Yet what can be a more effective way of giving people control of their own lives than to raise their awareness and arouse their energies through media they can relate to?

Popular communication is the most important educational tool for Africa. Popular communication can become a reality when it focuses on awakening the slumbering powers within the people. The possibilities of such an awakening can be terrifying to the people themselves and even to the rulers of Africa. When people wake up to the possibility of expressing their struggles, their conflicts, their hopes and fears, their aspirations and their abilities, they gain for themselves prophetic audacity. They become willing to dare to speak and to accept the consequences that come with speaking out.

For the masses of Africa, who do not have too much to protect, popular communication can be and has been embraced without great difficulty. It should not be any wonder that the authorities will do everything in their power to curb popular efforts. A strike of laborers is more frightening than that of medical doctors.

When the people of Soweto, for example, refuse to use those minibuses provided by the government and instead prefer to walk to their destinations, a communication event is taking place! It is being dramatized in the theater of daily life. It is evidence of an awakened people, a people aware of where they are coming from, where they are now, and where they could go! African leaders are not willing to come to terms with this type of challenge.

People's Theater

I want to illustrate the statements above by drawing on an example from Kenya. In 1976–77 the Kenyan novelist Ngugi Wathiong'o set up a community education and cultural center in a very small village called Kamiriithu. The village is inhabited by poor peasants, farmers, factory workers, mainly from a Bata shoe factory in a nearby small town called Limuru, plantation workers from large farms owned by rich people, and primary school teachers.

Ngugi Wathiong'o organized the village people, and they built a two-thousand–seat capacity open-air theater. Collectively they arranged for rehearsals to fit in with the working rhythm of the village, which meant meetings on Saturday and Sunday afternoons. Working together they created a play, which Wathiong'o and others scripted in their own local language. In 1977, they performed their first play, *Ngaahika Ndeenda* ("I Will Marry When I Want"). News about the theater soon hit the press, making headlines. Thousands of ordinary people from nearby villages and not a few from other parts of the country trekked to see the show. Some began to make inquiries about how to start similar theaters in their villages. After ten performances, the play was stopped by the Kenya government.

In February 1982, the same group attempted to perform another play, *Maitu Njugira* ("Mother, Sing for Me"), at the National Theatre, but the state authority refused to give them permission. They did, however, hold open-air rehearsal performances at the University of Nairobi. I was among thousands present at one of those rehearsals. The authorities quickly banned all such rehearsals, and all those associated with the Kamiriithu theater and the education center were either detained or fled the country.

Ngugi Wathiong'o was at the time an already accomplished novelist and a university professor. He had taught at the University of Nairobi for many years. His books were being used as high school and university texts in Kenya, elsewhere in Africa, and abroad. I not only studied Ngugi's books in school but also was one of his literature students at the university. Ngugi taught us to strive for an education that does not end with a degree. He wanted us to see the university as just one possible arena for learning. He forced us to see ourselves in the context of communities and not just as individuals. We began to see our aged grandparents as professors too, as we were sent to the villages to study under them and afterward to acknowledge them in our essays. We also learned about street children, beggars, and workers. Our class was used for testing out the ideas about popular theater. We were encouraged to come up with original thinking and to experiment with our ideas. Not once were we allowed to criticize anything or anybody without identifying with the problem and helping to come up with a solution.

Apparently Ngugi's preoccupation with university students did not raise the eyebrows of the rulers. It was his involvement in the community theater with masses of village people that earned him the wrath of Kenyan authorities. At the university he had access to only a few of us. He definitely occupied the role of a professor. He taught us in English. In the village, he was just another participant. The people had not read his books because they were written in English. Many of them had seen him grow up eating the same food as they did, and they still lived with him. Ngugi had chosen not to move into a university house but to commute from his village not far from the city of Nairobi. Ngugi also had chosen not to adapt to the white-collar "uniform" of ties and suits. He always dressed simply, and I must say most of the time he did not look very tidy. But this way of dressing enabled him to merge well with the working people of his village.

Ngugi tried and succeeded in mobilizing popular communication. The people were foremost involved in a process of thinking about their own lives and doing so in a language they understood best. Unfortunately, the authorities in Kenya never let the seed of this experiment with people's theater grow. The president of the republic made public speeches saying that the Kamiriithu theater group was practicing and teaching politics under the cover of culture. On March 10, 1982, the provincial commissioner, fully dressed in his colonial British uniform and accompanied by the whole of his security army, drove to Kamiriithu Community Centre to officially close it. He said that the people were being misled into cultural activities that had nothing to do with development. On the day that followed the similarly uniformed district commissioner led truckloads full of heavily armed police to demolish the Kamiriithu people's open-air theater. The majority of the actors had been women, youth, and workers. The theater had also pulled together a number of jobless teenagers and given them roles. Some were beginning to discover a potential they never knew they had. All of those who had found joy and hope as participants in a communication event were thrown back to step one. Today, only ten years later, this is one of the most dangerous places in the country in terms of crime. There is no proof that things would have been different if the Kamiriithu center had not been closed, but we can speculate.

The checks and balances that support a democratic society allow for tolerance and corporate respect for dissenting opinions. These are still a sweet dream for "the wretched of the earth."

JESUS THE REALIST
Tokunboh Adeyemo

Some thirty years ago, our continent, Africa, fought relentlessly against a common enemy called "colonialism." Our national political leaders, most of whom were products of Christian mission schools, were agitators in their youth, always busy arguing constitutional matters with colonial secretaries and governors. They were filled with dynamism and determination to free their people from sociopolitical oppression and to unite the shattered fragments of a bitterly divided continent from which they dreamed to create an earthly paradise.

The brave efforts and commendable sacrifice of such men as the Nobel Peace Prize winner, the late Kwame Nkrumah of Ghana; the late father of the Kenyan nation, Mzee Jomo Kenyatta; the late

---

Dr. Tokunboh Adeyemo is the general secretary of the Association of Evangelicals of Africa and Madagascar (AEAM). Printed in the booklet *Africa at a Crossroad,* this address was given to mark the Silver Jubilee anniversary of the AEAM (1966–91). Used by permission of the AEAM.

founder of Zaire, Patrice Lumumba; and the heads of state Mwal-
imu Julius Nyerere (Tanzania), Kenneth Kaunda (Zambia), Kamuzu
Banda (Malawi), Leopold Senghor (Senegal), Nnamdi Azikwe (Nigeria), and Houphouet-Boigny (Ivory Coast) can never be forgotten
in African history. Their vision was for one free Africa. Such men
and women had not much time to be young because no sooner
had the struggle for independence ended than the responsibility of
managing new nations was laid upon them. Within the space of
thirty years, a duration unparalleled for its brevity in the world's
political history, all foreign flags in Africa were replaced with national flags, while majority democratic rule is just around the corner
in South Africa. We salute the heroes and heroines of African
nationalism.

It was the general expectation of all Africans that attainment
of political independence would terminate the people's sufferings
and usher in an era of prosperity. In fact, with good intention,
Nkrumah preached: "Seek ye first the political kingdom and all else
will be added unto you." Probably a good percentage of the heads
of state who signed the Organization of African Unity (OAU) Charter at Addis Ababa, Ethiopia, in 1963 shared similar dreams. Since
the attainment of political independence, significant strides have
been taken in such areas as education, medical care, housing, food
production, and roads. However, without despising the value of self-
government and political freedom, we are living witnesses that it is
not all the answer. Today, far from being a paradise, Africa has been
described variously as "a bleeding continent" by President Moi of
Kenya, a "lost continent" by the International Monetary Fund, a "re-
tarded continent" by Ali Mazrui. Have you any future, Africa? Where
will you be by the year 2000?

The Pessimist's View

The pessimist sees nothing but deepest darkness. Politics in Africa
means power. Political independence brought a lot of power, but
ironically it came and remains, not in the hands of the people, but
in that of a small elite. The dream of creating a paradise has not only
been dashed, but turned into a nightmare in some places. Numerous
military coups have done nothing for Africa but retard its economic
development, while unschooled national leaders make mockery of
its institutions of higher learning. In a society of "the winner takes
all," failure to ally with the powers-that-be spells doom of detention
without trial, exile, or death. A famous Nigerian musician, Fela Kuti,

referred to African VIPs as "vagabonds in power." "With such lead-ers," reasoned the late Ugandan playwright Okot P'Bitek, "there can be no hope for Africa."

Whatever gain was made at independence has been lost through ignorance, mismanagement, carelessness, and personal greed. Take, for example, the currency of any nation in Africa. The strongest of them has been devalued not less than ten times since independence. While oil wells are regarded as a blessing in other parts of the world, they seem to be a curse in Africa. The common people are gripped by poverty across their nations. Traditional poverty largely caused by severe climatic environment and inappropriate technology has been accelerated by external forces, for example, of Structural Ad-justment Programs, the multinational companies, the debt crisis, and the African economies' inability to penetrate the international market economy.

In a situation of political instability and uncertainty, chronic eco-nomic recession, and financial hardship, one is not surprised to see the constant mass exodus of African professionals as well as a corresponding decrease of foreign investors.

Technologically, Africa is said to be stagnant. Though its lakes breed fish of all sorts and its forests all kinds of trees, Africa still imports sardines and toothpicks in large quantities. When the rest of the world is talking about faxes and computers, Africa is battling with manual typewriters.

African cities are bursting at the seams. For many school drop-outs from the rural area, going to the city is like going to paradise. In spite of escalating unemployment, shattered dreams, and unrealized expectations, the influx is not abated. Meanwhile, urban infrastruc-tures are overstretched and terribly inadequate, and traditionally stable rural life is threatened with collapse.

"To all this structural injustice," concludes the pessimist, "I add abuse of the judiciary, denial of human rights, unwanted street chil-dren, drought and famine, and the AIDS epidemic, and it is difficult for me to see any future for Africa." In fact we can say of Africa: "The harvest is past, the summer is ended, and we are not saved" (Jer. 8:20).

The pessimist's view of Africa is an accurate human socio-economic and political analysis of the continent. The facts are stark and cannot be denied. The main problem of this view—shared by a majority, including many Christians—is that it is a view from below. God is left out completely or even positioned against Africa.

The Optimist's View

The second view is that of an African who lives in a fool's paradise. It is the view of a blind nationalist who asserts proudly: "My country right or wrong," who has no room for engaging in any constructive criticism. It says of Africa, "Eat, drink, and be merry," but stops short of adding, "for tomorrow you shall die." An optimist casts a look at African forests, waters, minerals, oil reserves, and solar energy and says: "As it was in the beginning, is now, and ever shall be, world without end." There is an attitude of indifference to global ecopolitical issues in the guise of nonalignment.

The optimists consider population explosion as a myth or a ploy of the Western world. So they continue to multiply.

Optimists live in the past. They pride themselves on the ancestral traditions, the achievements of the freedom fighters, and Africa in diaspora. Rather than accept responsibility for national faults, optimists usually look for scapegoats from outside. As a result, colonial rule is still blamed for thirty years of mismanagement and fraud.

A pessimist and an optimist are psychological first cousins. While the former is a prisoner of circumstance, the latter is a prisoner of history. Neither of the two positions is acceptable to us. Is there an alternative? Yes. Looking at Africa through the eyes of Jesus—this is a realist's view!

The Realist's View

As evangelicals we identify with the realist's view. Prayerfully, we look at Africa through the Bible. "Arise, shine [Africa]; for your light has come, and the glory of the Lord has risen upon you" (Isa. 60:1). Africa used to be called a "dark continent." That was the time when the Prince of Persia—Satan—had dominance over Africa. Such evil practices as human sacrifice, witchcraft, sorcery, spiritism, and idolatry were rampant. Spiritually speaking, Africa was dead in sins. But as the Bible says, "Those who lived in a land of deep darkness—on them light has shined" (Isa. 9:2). The gospel of Jesus Christ has brought light and life to Africans in their millions. All reliable church-based statistics (including those of David Barrett, Patrick Johnson, and Larry Pate), indicate that by the year 2000, three-fifths of the world's more than two billion Christians will live in Africa, Asia, and Latin America—with Africa recording the highest numbers.

Speaking of realism, however, we must heed the warning of

About the AEAM

The Association of Evangelicals of Africa and Madagascar (AEAM), created in 1966, comprises national evangelical fellowships from twenty-one countries.

The AEAM statement of beliefs and commitments is:

We believe in the Holy Scriptures, as originally given by God, divinely inspired, infallible, entirely trustworthy and the supreme authority in all matters of faith and conduct. We believe in one God, eternally existent in three Persons: Father, Son and Holy Spirit. We believe in our Lord Jesus Christ, God manifest in the flesh, His virgin birth, His sinless human life, His divine miracles, His vicarious and atoning death, His bodily resurrection, His ascension, His mediatorial work, and His personal return in Power and Glory.

We believe in the salvation of lost and sinful man through the shed blood of the Lord Jesus Christ, by faith apart from works, and regeneration by the Holy Spirit. We believe in the Holy Spirit, by whose indwelling the believer is enabled to live a holy life, to witness and work for the Lord Jesus Christ. We believe in the spiritual unity of all those who, having believed in Jesus Christ for their salvation, have been regenerated by the Holy Spirit and compose therefore the church, the Body of Christ of which He is Head. We believe in the bodily resurrection of all the dead; of the believers unto everlasting blessedness and of the unbelievers unto judgement and everlasting punishment.

Based upon the Word of God and the command of our Lord Jesus Christ, we exist:

1. To promote evangelical unity and cooperation (John 17:21–23; Eph. 4:4–6)

2. To provide a platform for fellowship and partnership in the Gospel (Phil. 1:5)

3. To defend and confirm the Gospel against all forms of humanistic ideologies and theological liberalism (Phil. 1:7)

4. To further the Gospel, serving as a catalyst for world evangelization (Phil. 1:12)

5. To promote behavior and conduct consistent with the Gospel in humility, compassion and social justice under the Lordship of Christ (Phil. 1:27)

6. To render special services to all men, especially those of the household of faith (Gal. 6:10)

General Assemblies were held in 1969, 1973, 1977, 1981, 1987, and 1993. The governing body of the AEAM is the General Council, whose members include elected regional leaders and association representatives. The work of the AEAM is carried out from the headquarters in Nairobi, Kenya.

Dick France: "African Christianity needs more than numbers. It is a credulous church, wide open to any appealing new teaching that can quote a biblical verse or promise a miraculous healing to support its teaching. It needs more teaching and direction from within, not from without. It needs theology, its own African Christian theology. Until it has it, while it may continue to grow in numbers, it will not grow in influence on the new Africa, and it will be increasingly dismissed as a hangover from the colonial past."

We can't dismiss this advice. How many of us remember President Milton Obote's remark on the eve of Ugandan independence in 1962? He said: "Had it not been for the revolutionary teaching of the church concerning justice, Uganda would not have achieved its independence when it did." He went on to plead with the church not to sit back and congratulate itself, letting the new nation take its own course without guidance. People who know the history of Uganda since independence have blamed its woes partly on the church's withdrawal from its prophetic role as salt and light. The same could be said of other nations. Politicians have managed to shut Christians out, telling them not to mix church with politics—as if life could be so neatly dichotomized. The church of the 1990s must reject this lie.

We need Christians at the highest levels of national policy-making establishments. The church must intensify its revolutionary teaching on justice for all and its service of compassion to the poor, the widows, the orphans, and the destitute. It is righteousness that exalts a nation.

Quantity (number) must go hand in hand with quality (moral excellence). The Master didn't send us to win souls, but to make disciples, teaching them to observe all that he commanded. Discipleship involves evangelism and social responsibility. It has the far-reaching implication of holism of Luke 4:18-19. The church is mandated to reproduce Jesus Christ among all the peoples of the world. And we have no right to reduce the assignment to what we call "world evangelization." The influence of the church in society must match its number—as an agent of change. Sociologists say that it takes only 2 percent of a population to change it. If this is true, we ask, Where is Christian influence in Africa?

In the execution of its mission, the church will be opposed, hated, and persecuted. Nothing abnormal in this. After all, the Master has predicted: "In the world you face persecution. But take courage; I have conquered the world" (John 16:33). As the grazing zone between Christianity and Islam (namely, African traditional religion) diminishes, toleration will give way to confrontation such as Nigeria has gone through in recent days.

The realist, with whose view I identify completely, declares: "Not by might, nor by power, but by the spirit of the Lord of hosts" (Zech. 4:6). The realist sees Africa's spiritual, socioeconomic, moral, and political problems as a gigantic and unmovable mountain, but through the eye of faith in Jesus. By faith, the realist shouts: "What are you, O great mountain? Before the servant of the Lord you will become a plain." By faith, the realist confronts Africa of the 1990s with the love of Christ in the marketplace, the highway and byway, the corridors of power, the hall of justice, the *matatus* (public vehicles), and all over.

Realists don't withdraw from society into a cozy religious ghetto. Neither do they blindly plunge into the sea without adequate investigation, i.e., what the Bible terms as "counting the cost" (Luke 14:28). Like Joseph, realists know that years of leanness often follow years of great abundance. So they wisely save (Gen. 41). Like Daniel, realists resolve right from the onset not to defile themselves with the king's wine and food (Dan. 1:8). Like Esther, realists stand their ground in the struggle for justice, saying: "If I perish, I perish" (Esther 4:16). Like the three Hebrew children, realists side with God rather than bowing down to gods of gold and silver (Dan. 3). Like Paul, realists remember that only godliness with contentment brings great gain, while love of money plunges people into ruin and destruction (1 Tim. 6:6-10).

Realists don't romanticize the problems and challenges of life; neither do they ignore them. Instead they confront life's vicissitudes by faith in God. By faith and prayers, Christians not only tap heaven's resources, but also involve the supernatural directly in the affairs of their families, friends, relatives, and nations. With God as our Senior Partner in the prayer business, nothing shall be impossible. With faith in God the realist sings: "If you believe and I believe and we together pray, the Holy Spirit will come down and Africa shall be saved."

Africa by the year 2000—where shall it be? The answer depends upon the people of God. The future of Africa is not in the hands of secular politicians, economists, developers, financial institutions (with all of their good intentions), but in our hands as women and men of God and of prayer. Jesus is the only hope for Africa!

6

African Religious Traditions

INDIGENOUS RELIGION AND CULTURE
Jane Mutambirwa

In most African societies, interpretations of moral order, codes of ethics, and normal behavior at the individual, family, community, clan, or society level have their origin in traditional religion and culture. This essay focuses on religious beliefs and cultural values that have an impact on the lives of Africans, especially women. These perspectives are based on community cultures, especially among the Bantu peoples.

The Life Cycle

In indigenous religion, the human life cycle begins at conception and lasts into eternity. The person consists of the body of flesh, the mind-soul, and the spirit. The body is incapable of satisfying its instincts like hunger or thirst without the mind-soul giving it direction or instruction. This is why the body perishes after the mind-soul leaves at death.

The mind-soul is the system of cognitive processes, namely, thinking, planning, perceiving, and deciding on behalf of the person or personality. These qualities are believed to continue functioning after the body's death. Elders in the southern African region say, "The person or life does not perish."

From the moment the mind-soul is released from the body its cognitive processes acquire supernatural abilities. This is why a person in spiritual form is believed to see people's thoughts and to hear the most secret and isolated conversation. In a question on family care respondents said, "When passing the graves of family elders, women must bring children down from their backs and let them walk in single file for their elders to see."

Dr. Jane Mutambirwa is lecturer and coordinator for Behavioral Science and Studies in Family Health at the University of Zimbabwe School of Medicine. She delivered this paper at the Concerned Women Theologians Consultation in Manzini, Swaziland, in March 1992. The workshop was organized by the Ecumenical Documentation and Information Centre for Eastern and Southern Africa (EDICESA), in collaboration with the Council of Churches of Swaziland.

91

The spirit is the conscience of a person, which can keep activities and behavior moral and just. It is the inhibiting and restraining aspect of personality. It does not impose its function on a person; through thinking, planning, and deciding, persons can choose to let conscience direct or not direct their behavior. In other words a person can silence the voice of conscience.

The spirit, or conscience, is viewed as an attachment to the human personality. Elders in Shona culture say that "the souls of creatures and domestic animals do not reach the Creator." The Creator is believed to have added conscience to personality so that the mind-soul of human beings could live eternally and avoid *kufirira* (total death, or obliteration), which awaits the souls of other creatures after death of the body.

Eternal life is achieved by people who die after their mind-souls have reached spiritual maturity. Spiritual maturity is reached when conscience becomes permanently associated with the thinking, planning, perceiving, and deciding activities of a person's mind-soul. The process toward spiritual maturity is believed to begin with the first pregnancy and delivery. A couple learns to sacrifice personal needs for the sake of the expected child. After the first child-bearing, parents no longer live for themselves but are guided by conscience. At this stage a parent can protect the lives and guard the health of offspring and other forms of creation. It is believed that a person who goes through child-bearing will ensure that all other forms of creation are morally, justly, and fairly treated.

After the death of the body, the mind-soul of a person who has attained spiritual maturity is assured admission into the spirit world through the purification ceremony. During the purification ceremony the mind-soul is believed to become permanently integrated with conscience until eternity. At this stage the conscience-guided soul is said to protect the lives and guard the health of offspring in the same way that parents do in physical life. (Compare this with the role assigned to guardian angels or St. Christopher.)

The Roles of Family Members

It is believed in traditional religion that the Creator assigned the responsibility of passing on life from generation to generation to the male species. Life here means the sperm, commonly referred to as the "seed." Meanwhile women were assigned the responsibility of fertilization and nurturing life. The female role is equated to that of the soil.

The traditional family unit consists of grandparents, father and mother, and children. The grandfather is at the top of the hierarchy, the spiritual leader of the family. He and all male members of the family are responsible for molding the spiritual aspects of the family offspring and are regarded as the child's voice of conscience. Mothers often say to a mischievous child, "Wait until your father gets home."

Male members of the family are responsible for the overall protection of life. Sudden deaths and cancers or other diseases that threaten to terminate "the seed" before spiritual maturity are associated with lack of protection by the paternal line.

The grandmother is at the top of the female hierarchy. She and all female members of the family are responsible for molding the child's physical behavior, for example, how to hold a morsel of food or spoon, and social behavior, for example, how to develop interpersonal relationships. Female members of the family are responsible for protecting the child from physical and social harm. Any health problems associated with fertility and nurturing are believed to arise from lack of protection by the maternal line.

Life and health are believed to be protected by family members in the spirit world who continue to correct the behavior of their descendants. After death people are believed to continue to function according to their social and spiritual roles in physical life.

In Shona religious belief, life is a gift from the Creator, given in a state of absolute purity. Children are born spiritually and morally pure and stay that way until after puberty, that is, from conception to puberty children's souls are without sin. It is said that before puberty children cannot, of their own, contract diseases or illnesses. The birth of a child with a handicap or deformity is associated with some immoral or unhygienic act committed by parents or close family members. (Compare this with the Hebrew belief cited in John 9:2, which says: "His disciples asked him, 'Rabbi, who sinned, this man or his parents, that he was born blind?' ")

Children are believed to become ill only when custodians of their health and life breach morality or fail to follow spiritual hygiene that promotes health. For example, the father of the child who falls ill after the naming ceremony is asked to confess his misdemeanors and carry out the appropriate cleansing. Even during the illness the child's constitution continues to be considered as pure.

The child ceases to be spiritually pure after puberty. It is believed that the process of puberty stimulates the minds of youths to think immoral and impure thoughts about sex. The body is also perceived to become physiologically impure by going though menarche for girls and puberty for boys. The mind-soul of a person who departs from earth in this state cannot reach the spirit world or the Creator. Such a mind-soul suffers *kufiririra* (absolute death or obliteration), the most dreaded death in traditional religion and thought. For this reason, spiritual or moral hygiene for the soul is viewed far more seriously than physical hygiene for the body, which perishes after physical death.

Marriage and Procreation

The reproductive function of men is viewed as close to that of the Creator; elders in Shona society refer to the birth of a son as that of a *sika rudzi* (creator of the clan). Men are therefore viewed as endowed with a spiritually higher function than women. The role of women as recipients of the "seed" gives them a lower but more practical status in family life. Traditional marriage in Shona society is in three parts and consolidates these roles and functions in the following way.

The **dowry** entitles a husband to bodily pleasures with his wife and whatever she gains from physical work. It is difficult for a woman in African society to refuse to sleep with her husband or to share her earnings even when she knows that he is promiscuous and spending money on other women. The wife has the same right to both physical pleasures and earnings from her husband. As the parent responsible for physical and social well-being of the family, however, her needs are often subordinated to the practical realities that this role imposes on her in the home.

The **head of cattle** entitles the husband the right to his seed, i.e., the children in a marriage. The cows are sent to a girl's parents as advance appreciation payment for the womb that will house, fertilize, and nurture the seed. There should be one cow for each pregnancy, including miscarriages. The man who has more children than the cows he paid is asked to make more payments. Similarly the parents of a woman who has fewer pregnancies than were paid for are asked to return the balance to the husband.

The **binding ceremony** symbolizes the binding of the two families joined in marriage by an expected child. Conducted during or after the first pregnancy, this ceremony cements the marriage union. It is for this reason that traditionally a barren woman brought her sister, cousin, or brother's daughter as second wife to bear children on her behalf. Similarly, the family of a man who is impotent arranges for a brother to fertilize his wife on his behalf. Furthermore a widow who remarries feels that she needs to give the new husband a child even if she has children from her previous marriage.

Life after Death

Bodily death in indigenous religion does not mean the ultimate end of human life. The intangible and nonphysical mind-soul and spirit are believed to gain eternal life and maintain perpetual close association with the living members of their families. Eternal life is effected by traditional burial rites for the people whose mind-souls reach spiritual maturity before death of the body. There are three procedures: burial of the body, the cooling of the mind-soul, and the purification and integration of the mind-soul with the spirit or conscience.

It is customary for persons to state their desired place of **burial of the body** before death. If this request is not met, the "dark shadow" of the deceased can interfere with the preparation for putting the deceased person to rest.

The most rigid rite for burial is associated with married women. A married woman must not be buried before her father or a senior member of her father's household views her *chiso* (visage). She must be positively identified for admission into the ranks of ancestor spirits in the spirit world.

On the day of burial, pole bearers rest the bier on the ground at strategic points on their way to the grave. This is said to help the deceased person's mind-soul to maintain awareness of his or her surroundings. Landmarks of cleared ground on the way to the burial place are said to be for guiding the person back home after the purification ceremony.

Mourning is permitted only up to a point before the grave. Uncontrolled grieving is said to delay the deceased person's entry into the spirit world. After the burial people wash with malodorous medicines to get rid of the illness and to make it impossible for the "dark shadow" of the deceased to scent its way back home before the purification rites.

The **cooling period,** from the burial to the day of purification, is the time the mind-soul needs to become adjusted to its new form of existence. During the cooling period the spirit or conscience is symbolized by the "white shadow," which returns to other spirits as an outsider and waits to be united with its mind-soul on the day of the purification rites.

The mind-soul is viewed as existing without conscience during the cooling period. It is lonely and vulnerable to the selfish and aggressive tendencies of the body that it dominated during physical life. For this reason, people fear retaliation for misdeeds committed against a person before his or her death.

It is believed that the mind-soul of the deceased has a legitimate right to come home and haunt living members of the family for unnecessary delays in conducting the purification ceremony, which ends the deceased person's isolation and loneliness. Isolation and loneliness are viewed in the same way that Christians view hell.

Once cause of death has been established, beer for the ceremony is brewed and the **purification rites** are conducted according to the ethnic customs of the area. The mind-soul of the deceased is permanently integrated with the spirit or conscience and is escorted home from the grave by a procession of people joyfully dancing to warlike victory songs accompanied by the soft beat of drums. The mind-soul of the deceased person is considered to have conquered, gaining eternal life or continued existence in the spirit world. This is the person referred to as an ancestor spirit.

The ancestors are believed to be primarily concerned with the welfare of their descendants. When good things of life are realized people say, "The ancestors are with us" (*abaphansi banathi*). When misfortunes happen they say, "The ancestors are facing away from us" (*abaphansi basifulathele*), for the ancestors are believed to withdraw their protection and gifts of good fortune from erring descendants. Without their protection the descendants become vulnerable to all sorts of misfortune and diseases. Ancestors' spirits play a significant role in influencing indigenous people's outlook toward life, health, and nurture.

•

To date very little sound information exists on indigenous religious beliefs and their impact on the lives of African women. There is urgent need for teams of men and women to conduct studies from a religious perspective that address and identify solutions to the problems that women face from day to day. It is from such studies that appropriate parallels between indigenous and Christian religious beliefs can be identified and used in education for the liberation of women in African society.

AFRICAN INDEPENDENT CHURCHES: A MIGHTY MOVEMENT
M. C. Kitshoff

One of the remarkable phenomena in Africa is the rise and rapid growth of an indigenous church movement, known as the African Independent Churches. The AICs have developed into a mighty movement, bringing with them much of African religious tradition and adapting themselves to an Africa in transition. They have become places where Africans can feel at home. The AICs are described by Harold Turner as "having been founded in Africa by Africans, for Africans to worship God in African ways, and to meet African needs as Africans themselves feel them."

Phenomenal Growth

The AICs have proliferated in many countries but nowhere to the extent that they have in southern Africa. Here they emerged during the last few decades of the nineteenth century and experienced a rapid growth after World War II. Whereas in 1913 there were 32 known independent churches in South Africa, by 1980 the AICs had grown to include 3,270 denominations with a total membership of nearly six million. It is possible that at present South Africa could harbor well over 4,000 African independent denominations with no fewer than eight million adherents, representing between 35 and 40 percent of the African population. It is conceivable that the AICs could claim a membership of twelve million by the end of this century. If religion is relevant and a force to be reckoned with, these figures, though approximate, certainly provide evidence of the actual and potential power of this self-generating movement.

A variety of factors led to the AICs, including the phenomena of social change, industrialization, and urbanization; the relationship between black and white; Western denominationalism; a prohibitive and prescriptive missionary attitude; the lack of meaningful rituals in the historical churches; the need for small groups offering security and fellowship; traditional structures that stress decentralization; lack of other opportunities for black leadership; a search for African identity lost in the Westernized world; and the Bible.

M. C. Kitshoff is dean of the Faculty of Theology, University of Zululand, South Africa. This is an edited version of an article that first appeared in *South Africa International* 21, no. 3 (January 1991). Used by permission of the South Africa Foundation.

It might be surprising that the Bible, which advocates one new and eternal Kingdom, could be a factor leading to secession from one church and formation of another. Although the Bible emphasizes the value of the individual, the necessity for personal choice, concern for one's neighbor, and vitality and joy in worshiping God, not much attention was given to these by the mission churches. Moreover, the condemnation by missionaries of polygamy and the ancestor cult and their skepticism toward spirit-possession were questioned by black Christians, who found evidence in the Bible for their worldview.

Political Freedom and Freedom of the Spirit

In South Africa the birth of the AICs is usually associated with the secession led by Nehemiah Tile, a black minister of the Methodist Church in the Transkei. He founded the Thembu Church in 1884. He confronted white domination in both church and politics and held that an independent church was the only way in which black people could be true to themselves and become a nation. He not only advocated an indigenous interpretation of Christianity, but a view of blacks as rightful owners of Africa who should shed all control by the whites and determine their own affairs. He saw his church as a liberation movement to free the blacks from European control. By emphasizing a conception of "common blackness" he brought to the fore a new black consciousness, which would gather momentum during the twentieth century.

The independent churches that followed in Tile's wake were many and diverse. Two broad groups can be distinguished, namely, the Ethiopian-type and the Spirit-type.

The Ethiopian-type churches draw their name and inspiration from Psalm 68:31, where Ethiopia is implored to stretch out her hand to God. Ethiopia is believed to be the cradle of Christianity in Africa, and as an African state that has always retained its independence, it became a symbol of God's concern for Africa as well as a symbol of independence and freedom for Africans.

In 1892 Moses Mokone founded the Ethiopian Church in the Transvaal. Those who became leaders in the Ethiopian movement held Tile in high esteem for his opposition to racial inequality and socioeconomic and political injustices. Tile and Mokone laid the foundations of the Ethiopian movement, which played a significant role in the formation in 1925 of the African Native National Congress, which took over the task of working toward a South Africa where justice, human dignity, and equality would prevail.

The Spirit-type churches sprang from two movements, the Zionist movement and the Apostolic movement. As the Ethiopian-type churches emphasized ecclesiastical and political freedom in the African context, the Spirit-type churches stressed the freedom of the Spirit. The Zionist movement originated in South Africa in 1897. It was influenced by the Christian Catholic Church in Zion, established the previous year by John Alexander Dowie in the United States. Dowie had his own Zion City about forty-five miles from Chicago. His church stood for faith healing, rejection of medicine, abstinence from tobacco and alcohol, and adult baptism by immersion.

In 1902 a Dutch Reformed missionary, Pieter le Roux, joined the Christian Catholic Church in Zion, bringing with him his flock of four hundred Africans. In years to come millions were drawn from the African traditional religions into the Zionist churches, thereby creating the largest grouping of independent churches in South Africa.

Many of the Spirit-type churches identify themselves with Zion, referred to in the Bible as the mountain of Jerusalem and the place where God is revealed in power, glory, and mercy. For the Zionists, Zion is a symbol of spiritual strength and protection, and their own Zions, usually situated on hills, are places of spiritual fortification. Whereas the Ethiopian movement inspires and empowers adherents to overcome ecclesiastical, social, and political barriers in the quest for freedom, Zionism inspires and empowers adherents to find healing and spiritual freedom.

The Apostolic movement emerged in 1908 when an American, John Lake, established the Apostolic Faith Mission, which emphasized the outpouring of the Holy Spirit and speaking in tongues.

Probably 80 percent of the more than four thousand AIC denominations include "Zion" in their names, an indication that such churches give prominence to the work of the Spirit and to the practice of faith healing and speaking in tongues. That many African church names include "Zion," "Apostolic," and "Ethiopian" testifies to the fact that Zionists and Apostolics have much in common, demonstrating a process of cross-fertilization and ongoing proliferation of the AICs.

Communities of Healing

The Zionist and Apostolic churches practice healing as an integral part of their church activities. For Africans, health and healing are bound up with a harmonious adjustment to the visible and the invisible worlds. Illness is believed to result from a disturbance in balance between the human world and the spiritual world, e.g., from wrong deeds, malice toward society, or failure to perform certain rituals. On the other hand, health is defined in terms of self-fulfillment through harmony with the "life-force." The African approach to sickness and health is a holistic one: sickness strikes at the wholeness of the person in society with healing directed toward a quest for identity, total well-being, and a search for salvation in its widest sense.

Within this context, AICs naturally find themselves deeply involved in the process of healing. The healer, who often assumes the office of prophet, is seen to stand in a special relationship with the life source, as an intermediary between the profane and sacred worlds. Understanding of the illness and the power to heal emanate from the Spirit, *Umoya*, often assisted by ancestral spirits that are central to the healing process. For churches that accept Jesus Christ as the bringer of salvation, the Spirit that heals is the Spirit of Christ.

The healing procedure may include the use of water, ashes, staves, and clothing. Water is closely associated with the source of being, and sea water is seen as a source of power and energy. Every Sunday members of AICs can be seen on the Durban beach clothed in colorful uniforms. The sick person's social or church group is called upon to perform rituals to enhance health by singing, praying, speaking in tongues, and laying on of hands to emphasize that healing is a communal matter involving contact with the supernatural.

Participants experience healing, health, and wholeness, which confer individual worth in an urbanized and often depersonalized society. It is within the AICs as healing communities that the underprivileged and dispossessed African can say: "I am, because I count and am cared for," or, "I am only because we are, and since we are, I am."

Fortification against Evil Spirits

Witchcraft, sorcery, ancestor wrath, and spirit possession are basic elements in African cosmology, seeking to destroy life by means of misfortune, illness, and death. In modern terms the adversaries are identified as the evil forces of colonialism. Modernization, urbanization, social disruption, and personal disorientation have all caused tension and insecurity and can increase the people's fear of many unpredictable and unspecified forces.

The Bible takes the matter of spiritual adversaries seriously, as do the AICs, in line with the traditional African thought and belief pattern regarding evil spirits. In the AICs the emphasis is not on counterattacking evil forces but on fortifying members. This is achieved by preaching the scriptural message that God cares, by offering prayers, and by administering the sacraments. Members of the AICs also wear cords, stars, and beads and use ashes and candles to ward off the evil forces. These objects are believed to have powers that come either from God the Holy Spirit or "good" ancestor spirits. Traditional diviners and herbalists are also visited for additional protection.

The AICs, especially the Zionists, strongly oppose sorcery, and to counter the attacks of sorcerers inner cleansing is necessary. Washing and vomiting are seen to expel evil; vomiting is usually effected by drinking a mixture of sea water, or water with salt, and ashes. Prayers are offered and specific ritual procedures are followed.

Spirit possession, or *amafufunyama,* is an illness with a fairly standard pattern of symptoms. The spirit-possessed person exhibits antisocial behavior, extreme agitation, confusion, depression, lack of control, and destructiveness that may climax in unconsciousness with voices speaking from within the body. A woman may speak with a man's voice. Such symptoms are consistent with New Testament narratives of demon possession. Some of the AICs, especially the Zionists, thus are able to use a biblical model—prayer and reprimanding the spirit(s) in the name of Jesus—as a means of exorcism.

Caring for One Another

AICs are also involved in the important economic activities of voluntary mutual benefit societies such as savings clubs, lending societies, *stokvels* (informal savings funds), and burial societies.

These mutual aid societies have obvious socioeconomic benefits, but also a socioreligious dimension, usually in the form of worship where hymns are sung and prayers offered. In this way even non-church members are brought into the sphere of Christianity.

In African traditional society, mutual aid was a kinship and community responsibility. Industrialization and urbanization blazed the trail for individualism. The mainline churches were either indifferent or unable to respond meaningfully to the total needs of the African. The churches that separated from the mainline churches used mutual benefit societies as instruments of caring. They emerged in townships and cities to compensate for diminishing kinship care and as a means of self-expression and self-recognition in a restrictive society.

AIC members play a prominent role in burial societies, which enable impoverished people to bury their dead as their culture and religion demand. They fulfill financial, social, psychological, and spiritual roles in supporting the physical and emotional needs of the bereaved.

Mutual benefit societies reflect a holistic approach in caring for the needs of black people and are a dynamic expression of the consciousness of a caring African Christianity. They fulfill economic needs, teach members how to deal with money, and provide scope for black initiative and black leadership. They are exercises in democracy: all decide and all share. They are ecumenical and offer worship in a personalized environment. They work toward the improvement of the quality of life and build a sense of security.

Development and Progress

The AICs are opening avenues for economic development and personal progress. As the traditional worldview has gradually changed and people have come to see that nature can be controlled and that people can shape their own destinies and are not totally subject to controlling mystical forces, these churches have increasingly recognized a work ethic as a prerequisite for development. The AICs promote a simple lifestyle, free of alcohol and tobacco, and a philosophy of sharing. No claims for financial investment in church buildings or administration are made, and any income is largely used to assist needy fellow members. In this way, AICs are shifting the emphasis from consumption to provision and from reliance on the community to self-help. Some of these churches sponsor specific economical activities whereby new ideas and techniques are explored. In this sense, the AICs constitute a liberation movement endeavoring to free their people from poverty and subservience.

The Attraction

While the rise of the independent church movement involved centrifugal forces that made people leave Western-oriented churches, the growth of the AICs displays centripetal forces that bring people to these churches. Generally, the attraction of the AICs lies in their life-enhancing activities: the AICs are communities where people can share in a totality of relationships that enable them to participate in the fullness of being. People are attracted to the churches not necessarily because they are ill but because, as Africans, they are in search of health and well-being. According to the testimony of many adherents, they received "health" in the AICs.

Also, these churches take the negative forces within African cosmology seriously by responding to real problems as perceived by Africans, namely, witchcraft, sorcery, and evil spirits. They believe that it is quite natural to interpret socioeconomic hardships and deprivation in contemporary society in the context of adverse cosmic forces. The AICs, in particular the Zionists, are considered to be experts in granting people protection and fortification against the powers of evil.

Worship services are a further attraction. In the Spirit-type churches every service is an event with sensory appeals. The sermons are interspersed with dancing, singing, clapping of hands, ecstatic experiences, prophecies, and communal prayer. In these unsophisticated services, often held in homes and expressed in the African idiom, real fellowship is experienced. As voluntary associations fulfilling the role previously played by the kinship group in rural areas, these churches provide networks of security and identity in the urbanization process. A new family is created, extending much further than the traditional extended family.

The AICs and the Future

It is widely held that the future of the church in Africa belongs to the AICs, which are in the forefront of the spectacular growth of Christianity in sub-Saharan Africa, and specifically South Africa. What, however, is the quality of Christianity portrayed by the AICs? Can these churches be seen as Christian? Responses vary: "Some are and some are not." Such vague and open-ended answers are often interpreted as insulting and an expression of spiritual hubris. A more cautious approach would be to acknowledge varying levels of Christian understanding.

Concern has been expressed about the role of ritual in the AICs, especially ritual with the purpose of gaining or transferring "power" or "the Spirit." Some rituals are seen to associate AICs with magic or "superstition." For example, when water is blessed and used for baptism or healing purposes, it is generally accepted that the wholeness of water is internalized, resulting in a mysterious infusion of power and energy. The importance of adult baptism as a purification rite makes it conceivable that baptism could become the only requirement for admission to the AICs. A nominal but lifeless and even Christless Christendom could again present itself.

Another practice that arouses concern is that some AIC leaders develop into messianic figures, usurping the place of Jesus Christ. Further, preaching is often seen to be inadequately Bible-oriented and Christ-centered. A commonly held view is that Christ is seen as a magical personality and not as the Christ of the Bible. It is often difficult to distinguish between the functions of the Holy Spirit and the ancestor spirits. Finally, there is an impression that a large part of the movement sees the church as a cultic community, unaware that a Christian church finds its life and center in Jesus Christ.

It is, however, possible to assume a positive stance to the AICs. They have vitality and creativity in abundance, and most regard the Bible as having divine authority. When the unique Bible message is understood, accepted, and applied, the AICs in South Africa can become a leading movement in socioeconomic development and political renewal and progress. They teach a holistic approach to healing and demonstrate joyful fellowship in worship. In short, the AICs have the potential to help reconstruct South Africa into a country in which we can all feel at home.

REDEMPTION THEOLOGY FROM AN AFRICAN CONTEXT
Rosina Ampah

There are several meanings to the word "redemption" in the Bible. One, a legal concept found in the Old Testament, designates a process by which something alienated, or at least subject to alienation,

Born in Ghana, the Rev. Sister Rosina Ampah, O.S.H., is a member of the Order of St. Helena, a religious community for women in the Anglican Communion. This is an edited version of an essay she wrote while studying at New York Theological Seminary and is used by permission.

may in some circumstances be recovered for its original owner by the payment of a sum of money. The thing alienated may be either real property or an animal or the legally forfeit. In the Old Testament this root word is never used except with regard to the redemption of persons or other living beings.

Another root word is used for the theological concept of redemption in the Old Testament: since the essential purpose of a redemptive act is to deliver a person or thing from captivity or loss, it becomes an appropriate image for God's saving actions among humans. Against the background of Hebrew law, the image has a vividness that can hardly be realized by peoples of different background and culture. The concept of redemption could be applied to groups or to individuals who were in trouble.

In the New Testament, however, the use of the concept is very limited because of the difference in cultural background, which made other images such as Atonement, Sacrifice, and Justification more intelligible and appealing. Redemption in the New Testament always implies deliverance from sin and its effects, rather than merely from death or trouble.

With these explanations from both Old and New Testament I can formulate my own meaning of redemption as I understand it as a Christian and as an African. It is very hard to maintain a traditional theology of redemption when one gives serious thought to the crucifixion. It is hard to accept a loving father who would send a loving son to be executed in order for God to forgive the sins of God's own creation. On the other hand, one can make sense of the cross after Jesus' resurrection in the sense that the cross was a stepping stone to God's glory even though it was the world's wicked way of dealing with Jesus.

My own theology and understanding of redemption are based on deliverance from sin and its effects and bringing alienated people into relationship with God and with each other. For me, redemption happened not because Jesus was crucified on the cross, but rather because Jesus taught and showed the people how best to live their lives when he was still alive. Because of that teaching, he was falsely accused and killed. Again, the community of believers came together because Jesus made a difference in their lives and was willing to die an unjust death for their sake. Furthermore, Jesus socialized with people whom others thought were not good enough, and he helped them to become what God intended them to be. Jesus could have obeyed what the authorities had expected from him, but he chose not to, knowing that by disobeying them they might use force on him. This for me is the redeeming work of Jesus! It is his making the conscious choice of helping others to rebuild their broken relationship with God and with their neighbors, at the expense of his own life.

A redemption story told in my culture is an annual celebration for the whole Fante tribe, a coastal people in Ghana. The story goes like this: There was once a man named Ahor who lived in one of the villages in the Fante land. One year the gods of the land were upset with the people and sent out plagues among the inhabitants. People were dying like flies everywhere and there was nothing anyone could do to help them. One of the diviners was able to consult the gods on behalf of the people and found that the only action that would save the Fante tribe was sacrifice of a male virgin to the gods on behalf of the people. When a man named Ahor heard the requirement, even though he was the only child of his parents, he had pity on the Fante tribe and offered himself as a sacrifice to the gods. As soon as he was killed, the plague came to an end and the Fantes were saved; this is why the Fantes celebrate the *Ahobaa* festivals every year. The *Ahobaa* means *Ahor nabaa*—thanksgiving of honor to Ahor, whose generous self-giving saved the tribe. That is a redemptive story, and the celebration has been going on from generation to generation without fail in the Fante land. The celebration begins with mourning for Ahor (and family members who have died in the previous year), followed by celebration of joy for Ahor's victory over the plagues.

The story of Ahor is similar to that of Jesus' death. It was not so much the killing of Jesus on the cross that turned people's lives around, but the love and the integrity with which Jesus accomplished his death. I believe also that it was through this selfless love that God chose to raise Jesus up again from the dead.

As an African I find it easy to believe that Jesus' death was caused by the agent of evil rather than a loving God, just as Ahor's was. According to Kwesi A. Dickson of Ghana: "Death is caused by evil. The African understanding of causation is of relevance here: nothing happens that will not have been purposefully caused. Death invariably receives something more than a physical explanation. To be sure, physical explanations are understood, but the African would go beyond the physical to seek a theological explanation." Because Africans believe that the spiritual world is not separate from the physical world, all that brings suffering and deprivation is ultimately traceable to other than physical causes.

In a way, I understand Jesus' redeeming work much better in an African context since death in African societies affects a much wider social group than the deceased's immediate family. The rituals in connection with death serve to reaffirm the sense of solidarity of the larger group and to place the latter's support at the disposal of the bereaved. In the same way, Jesus' death affects that larger world; the re-enactment of the events reaffirms the solidarity of Christians throughout the world. Furthermore, the context of the death on the cross is humiliation, and since many Africans have suffered humiliation and shame, they can easily identify with the cross as a symbol. The cross demonstrates human degradation and evil, but it also demonstrates triumph.

According to Dickson, one can further Jesus' redeeming work through Jesus' mission by educating the people to live in relationship with God and with each other in community, family, congregation, and church — nurturing and challenging them with the gospel to be people of God, developing and using their full potential, thinking and acting responsibly, and serving in congregation and culture. Furthermore, Jesus' death on the cross enables people to live and help others live Christ-reconciled lives through acceptance and understanding of the gospel, both as a historic reality and as a living word of life, guiding and freeing persons, church, and society. That is the kind of redemption Jesus died for! Jesus died that we may have life and have it abundantly. He freed us from our burdens of guilt and shame. Jesus reconciled us to God and to each other, and that is the redemptive claim that I believe in, the wholeness from which I am free to die to the world in order to live for God and God's people. That is my theology of redemption, to believe in a God who is willing to go to the extreme in order to save the least of creation.

ISLAM AND CHRISTIANITY IN AFRICA
Johannes Haafkens

As we think about Islam and Christianity in Africa, it is of crucial importance to realize that Muslims and Christians belong to the same human community. Our belonging together as human beings is beautifully expressed in a sculpture called *Ujamaa,* made by artists in Tanzania. The sculpture, in the shape of a trunk of a tree, consists of a great number of human beings holding each other. They are all different but together form one trunk.

As Christians we belong to the one human family. Other members of this family are Muslims. As we all know, it is not wise to ignore family problems. They are to be faced, to be discussed openly and sincerely, with the purpose of maintaining the unity of the family.

Western scholars estimate the percentage of Muslims in Africa as a whole at 41.7 or 41.2 percent. The Islamic Foundation estimate is 58–59 percent. Like estimates for the individual regions of Africa, these estimates vary greatly depending on the source (see the chart on the next page). What conclusions can we draw from these data? With a population expected to reach 800 million around the year 2000, there is little doubt that by then there will be over 300 million adherents of Islam, and over 300 million adherents of Christianity on the continent. On the basis of these figures, one can safely say that Africa cannot be considered either a Muslim or a Christian continent. We all know that it is impossible to separate Christians and Muslims by moving each community to a separate geographical areas. It is therefore of the utmost importance that the adherents of the two religions should work together in a spirit of mutual respect to build a better future for Africa. A division of Africa along religious lines would have disastrous consequences.

The Muslim Community in Historical Perspective

In several parts of sub-Saharan Africa, the Muslim community came into existence more than a millennium ago. We know that around 615 C.E., during the lifetime of Prophet Muhammad, Muslim refugees from Mecca found protection in Aksum in Ethiopia with the

The Rev. Dr. Johannes Haafkens of the Netherlands is general advisor of the Project for Christian-Muslim Relations in Africa, headquartered in Kenya. This essay is condensed from his presentation to the AACC Symposium in Mombasa in 1991 and is used by permission.

	Total population (CHEAM*)	Muslim population (CHEAM)	Percentage of Muslims (CHEAM)	Percentage of Muslims (Islamic Foundation)†	Percentage of Muslims (WCE)‡	Percentage of Christians (WCE)
North Africa	93,476,000	87,778,000	94.0	95.8	91.2	8.5
West Africa	153,292,000	72,121,000	47.0	71.4	46.2	37.0
Central Africa	48,161,000	4,050,400	8.4	25–28	9.2	44.2
North East Africa	55,815,000	29,945,000	53.7	75	51.7	35.0
East Africa	83,690,000	11,206,000	13.4	35–37	13.4	62.6
Southern Africa	48,458,000	507,560	1.0	6–10	1.0	77.6
Indian Ocean	11,966,000	668,150	5.6	21–24?	5.6	50.8
Total Africa	494,858,000	206,276,110	41.7	58–59	41.2	44.2

* CHEAM (1981): *A Map of the Muslims in the World: Explanatory Summary with Statistic Tables*, conceived and produced by the Centre for Advanced Studies on Modern Asia and Africa (CHEAM), Paris, edited by R. Delval. *Explanatory Summary with Statistic Tables* (Leiden: E. J. Brill, 1984).

† Islamic Foundation (c. 1976): M. M. Ahsan, *Islam, Faith and Practice* (Nairobi: The Islamic Foundation, 1985), pp. 43–47; new revised edition of a work first published by the Islamic Foundation, U.K., in 1977).

‡ WCE (1980): *World Christian Encyclopaedia*, edited by David B. Barrett (Nairobi: Oxford University Press, 1982).

Christian king, the Negus. There has been a Muslim presence on the East African coast for more than a thousand years. In ancient Ghana (situated in present-day Mauritania, Senegal, and Mali), Muslims had considerable influence at the court of the king around the year 1000. In 1324, Mansa Musa, the ruler of ancient Mali, made the pilgrimage to Mecca. Islam became firmly established in Kano, in present-day Nigeria, in the second half of the fifteenth century.

In many areas, Islam spread through the activities of traders and clerics and through rulers who converted to Islam under their influence. Sufi orders played a significant role in making Islam accessible for African people. Important also were the reform movements, which advocated a purification of Islam on the basis of its Arabic sources: the Qur'an, the Traditions, and the *Shari'a* (the Islam code of conduct). In West Africa, for example, between 1700 and 1900, revolutionary movements led to the establishment of Islamic states. Rulers accused of being half-hearted Muslims, of disobeying the *Shari'a*, and concluding alliances with non-Muslims, were overthrown. Armed force was used to establish, maintain, and extend these states.

Colonial rulers generally adopted a pragmatic approach to Islam.

They tried to avoid antagonizing Muslims by maintaining and at the same time controlling traditional institutions. In strongly Muslim areas, they adopted a system of indirect rule in which Muslim rulers were left or put in charge of administration, for example, in northern Nigeria and on the East African coast. Some traditional rulers converted to Islam, for example, in the Bamoun area in Cameroon around 1917, and non-Muslim subjects of Muslim rulers became Muslim in several areas. Sufi orders extended their influence, for example, in Malawi. Muslim urban communities, involved in trade, crafts, and service to the colonial administration, attracted new members. An example here is the city of Nairobi in Kenya; before 1920, most of its inhabitants were Muslims.

New Institutions

In the twentieth century, a new type of institution came into existence. The Ansar ud-Deen Society, established in western Nigeria in 1923, was formed in accordance with the modern laws introduced to Nigeria by the British. It established mosques together with schools, following a curriculum set by the colonial government. English was the language of instruction; Islam provided the religious aspect of the program. Such modern Muslim schools became more and more numerous. In 1964, for example, a Muslim Girls Grammar School was established in Ibadan, Nigeria, by a Muslim women's society.

The need to provide students with books on Islam in English led to the production of Islamic literature in English by the Islamic Publications Bureau in Lagos and the Islamic Foundation in Kenya. English translations of the Qur'an, printed alongside the original Arabic text, are widely distributed by Muslim organizations, as are classical sources of Islam, such as the main collections of the Prophetic traditions.

The traditional Qur'an school, where children learned to recite the Arabic Qur'an by heart and later got an opportunity to study some of the centuries-old basic Arabic works on Islam, prepared its students for life in the traditional Muslim African society. The books in English intend to provide guidance for life in modern African society. A new understanding of Islam is developing here, affecting even the traditional Muslim concept of God. The emphasis is now more on human responsibility than on God's omnipotence.

The Influence of Christianity

The new Muslim organizations, including those actively pursuing mission work in Africa, the modern Muslim schools, the literature providing new interpretations or presentations of Islam — all these are to a certain extent a conscious response to the Christian presence. D. O. S. Noibi reports how in Western Nigeria Muslim youth organizations have been established as alternatives to existing Christian organizations; for example, the Council of Muslim Youth Organizations is a counterpart to the Youth Wing of the Christian Association of Nigeria, the Sheriff Guards is a Muslim version of the Boys Brigade. Dr. Noibi also reports that efforts by the Young Muslim Brothers and Sisters (YOUMBAS) in Ibadan to make recordings of Islamic songs were inspired by the fact that Christian songs have been attracting young Yoruba Muslims to Christianity. He also mentions that various Muslim organizations have developed wedding ceremonies very similar to those conducted in churches, because young Muslims have found such church ceremonies very attractive.

Modern Muslim missionary activity has been developed, at least in part, in response to Christian mission work in Africa. I still remember how around 1972 an Egyptian "missionary" in Cameroon expressed his admiration for the quality of education provided for future Christian leaders at the Protestant Theological Faculty in Yaounde. He observed that such good training institutions were not yet available for Muslims in Africa. An awareness of the existence of well-equipped Christian institutions is likely to have provided a stimulus for Muslims to strengthen Islamic educational facilities in Africa. We can think here of the development of programs for Arabic and Islamic studies in public universities and of the establishment of Islamic universities in Niger and Uganda.

The Affirmation of Muslim Identity

Despite a growing number of similarities between Islam and Christianity in Africa, Islam is not becoming a kind of "Unitarian" Christianity. Muslims have their own religious heritage to which they turn for inspiration. An important and distinctive element in this heritage is the *Shari'a,* the Law of Islam, its code of conduct that regulates individual and collective life. In its classical form it is concerned with worship as much as with family life, commerce, and the conduct of the affairs of state. In the last twenty years or so,

---

The Accidents of Religious Affiliation

In Nigeria Bishop S. O. Odutola and Bishop I. G. A. Jadesimi, the first two Anglican bishops from Ijebu Ode, were born into Muslim families. Bishop Sanusi, the first Catholic bishop in the Catholic diocese of Ijebu, was born into a Muslim family in Iperu. So was his successor, the present bishop. So was the first Ijebu man to be recruited into the Catholic priesthood, Fr. Sadiku. Chief Timothy Adeola Odutola, the nonagenarian Baba Egbe ("father of the group") of Ijebu Christians was born into a Muslim family; his younger brother, Chief Jimo Odutola, remained a Muslim.

What made the difference seems to have been schooling—the Qur'anic school or the missionary day school, literacy in the Arabic script or literacy in the Roman script, religious studies in an Oriental language or humanistic studies in a European language. Chief Timothy Adeola Odutola went to Ijebu Ode Grammar School, founded by Yoruba Anglican clergymen. His brother, Chief Jimo Odutola, did not. Jimo Odutola sent his sons to Ijebu Ode Grammar School and his daughters to Holy Child College, Lagos: the boys kept the religion of their father; the girls married Catholic men from St. Gregory's College and are staunch Catholic women today.

I am Anglican because my father went on from the United Native African Church Primary School, Phoenix Lane, Lagos, to the Church Missionary Society Grammar School on Odunlami Street, where he was presented for confirmation at the Cathedral Church of Christ. He was living with his elder brother, who was then a member of the Catholic Church. Their father back in Ijebu Ode had quit the Anglican Church rather than send away any of his five wives: he had joined the United Native African Church formed in 1891. By the time Christianity had reached our home town, my grandfather was already an adult. Such were the accidents of religious affiliation in the first three generations of Christianity in Nigeria, 1842-1942.

—*Modupe Oduyoye*

---

more and more voices have been heard within the Muslim community worldwide, emphasizing the importance of the *Shari'a* for the social, economic, and political life of human communities.

Another important development in the Muslim world has been the Organization of the Islamic Conference, formally established in 1971 following a summit meeting of Muslim heads of state in Rabat, Morocco, in 1969. An organization of governments, it highlights the role that Islam plays on the level of the state. The African members are: Egypt, Libya, Tunisia, Morocco, Algeria, Mauritania, Senegal, Guinea-Bissau, Guinea, Mali, Burkina Faso, Niger, Sierra Leone, Benin, Cameroon, Gabon, Chad, Sudan, Uganda, Djibouti, Somalia, and the Comoros. There has been controversy about Nigeria's membership.

Movements advocating a radical Islamization of society, generally called fundamentalist in the West, have been gaining ground in sub-Saharan Africa, especially since about 1975. Influences from other parts of the Muslim world play a definite role here.

However, changes in society in sub-Saharan Africa are a key factor. There is a widespread feeling that things are not as they ought to be in society. Both traditional and secular approaches are felt to be inadequate by many Muslims. Significant groups of people, among them young academics and business people, are therefore turning to modern radical interpretations of Islam. In northern Nigeria and Niger, the Izala movement, which opposes Sufism as well as secularism, is one example; the Islamic Front in Sudan is another. Claiming that only the *Shari'a* can provide a sound basis for human society, radical Muslims reject the consensus reached at independence in many African countries, which implied that the nation-state would be secular or neutral in religious matters.

Although the radical movements among Muslims are very vocal at the moment and have real influence in society, there are other shades of opinion among Muslims. It is important to note that the radicals oppose what they consider to be an undue Africanization or Westernization among fellow Muslims. Also, it is likely that sometimes the banner of radical Islam is used to further or defend political and economic interests of particular communities. Examples can be found in several countries, including Nigeria and Sudan.

Christian-Muslim Relations in Africa

Missionaries who came to Africa from Europe and America, influenced as they were by the centuries-long rivalry between Christianity and Islam in the Mediterranean area, considered Islam generally a danger for Christianity. Missionary strategists thought of setting up a barrier of mission stations to stop the spread of Islam to the south.

Although some written documents give the impression of considerable tension between Christians and Muslims, personal relations between missionaries and their Muslim neighbors have been respectful, even cordial in many cases. In the second half of the nineteenth century, Bishop Samuel Ajayi Crowther became a good friend of several Muslim rulers in Nigeria. In western Nigeria, Muslims who initially watched the advent of Christianity with caution

Islam Studies Neglected

Nigerian Christian theologians have studied African traditional religion more closely than they have studied Islam. In neglecting Islam and concentrating on African traditional religion, they are developing a dangerous blind spot as they pilot the boat of evangelism through the sea of religious pluralism, which is the context in which they preach. Whereas 45 percent of Nigerians are today Muslim, only about 10 percent base their life on traditional religion. When the missionaries in Southern Nigeria in the mid-nineteenth century decided to study traditional religion, almost 90 percent of the people of southern Nigeria lived by traditional religion. Church seminaries in particular need to wake up to this fact and respond more competently to the changes in their environment. The knowledge of Islam among Nigerian Christians is dangerously shallow.

It is also inexcusable. At the beginning of contact between Christian missionaries and Islam in Nigeria, the Christians borrowed vocabulary of a faith religion from the Muslims:

	Arabic	Yoruba Muslim Vocabulary	Yoruba Christian Vocabulary
"prayer"	´ad-duʷˋaa	àdúà	àdúrà
"preach"	waˋat		wàásù
"preaching"	ma-wᵉˋit-ah	wàásí	ì-wàásù
"clergyman"	haliyf-ah	ààfáà	àlùfáà
"pagan, unbeliever"	kaafir	kèfèrí	kèfèrí

In this early period, a Yoruba clergyman of the Church Missionary Society translated the Qur'an into Yoruba, the first such translation and the only one until about twenty-five years ago. A reading of Edward Blyden's *Christianity, Islam and the Negro Race* (published out of his experience in West Africa at the end of the nineteenth century) shows the high estimate of Islam that then prevailed among Christian clergymen.

—Modupe Oduyoye

and put up a sort of passive resistance, later became ready to engage in public discussions, which were generally good-natured, and grew less suspicious of modern education.

The newly won independence of many countries in sub-Saharan Africa around 1960 brought a new emphasis on national unity. Constructive cooperation between citizens of different linguistic, cultural, and religious backgrounds, forming together one nation, became a matter of the highest priority.

With independence, Protestant and Catholic circles became infected by the hope for a better future for Christians and Muslims together. Thus the importance of traditional African values concerning life in community was emphasized, as Christian theologians highlighted positive aspects of African culture and religion. There was an awareness of problems that might arise after independence in the Christian-Muslim relationship, but also a good measure of confidence that these could be overcome.

As a result of the new thinking about the Christian approach to Islam in Protestant circles, a process of consultation among churches and missions in Africa was initiated. This led, in 1959, to the establishment of the "Islam in Africa Project." The project emphasized Christian witness in a spirit of mutual respect and love, rather than in a spirit of confrontation and combat. It emphasized that the church, as it is called faithfully to interpret the gospel of Jesus Christ in the Muslim world, should try to come to a deeper understanding of its Muslim neighbors and their religion. Area committees organized seminars, published booklets, and launched a program to train more resource persons for the churches. The project continues to be active. In 1987 its name was changed to Project for Christian-Muslim Relations in Africa.

The hope that Christian-Muslim relationships would gradually improve and become more harmonious was confirmed by developments in the political field. The 1972 peace accord in Sudan envisaged peaceful coexistence of Christians and Muslims in a country that had been ravaged by civil war. The Nigerian Civil War (1967–70) did not lead to general polarization. Senegal, with a large Muslim majority, remained peaceful under a Christian president, Leopold Sedar Senghor. The conflict between Senghor and Mamadou Dia, another Muslim political leader, centered on the interpretation of socialism, Senghor being more pragmatic, Dia more radical. It was not seen as religious conflict.

Yet Christian-Muslim relations have proved to be more complex and more difficult than many had thought or hoped. Sudan and Nigeria can be mentioned as examples. The Sudan peace accord broke down in 1983 and the civil war started again. Although the political and cultural background of this conflict previously had been given much emphasis, the introduction of *Shari'a* laws by the Numeiri regime in 1983 has led to more focus on its religious dimension.

In Nigeria, tension between Christians and Muslims has been growing since 1977, when a debate started about the place of the *Shari'a* in the constitution of the country. This tension led to out-

breaks of violence and loss of human life on several occasions.
While the religious dimension of violent conflicts has been emphasized both in Sudan and in Nigeria, it is important not to lose sight
of the underlying economic, social, and political factors at work on
both the national and international levels.

A Common Agenda

As Christians, we are called to work for the unity of the communities, the nations, to which we belong. Christians and Muslims
are called, together with others, to find solutions for the many
problems that confront Africa today. From our different religious
backgrounds, we share a concern for the orphan and the widow,
for those marginalized in human society. Christians and Muslims
can work together for justice and peace, for respect for God's
creation. Many efforts have already been made to enhance such cooperation. We mention here as examples the encounters between
African Christians and Muslims organized by the World Council of
Churches in 1986 in Porto Novo, Benin, and 1989 in Arusha, Tanzania, in which such themes as "Religion and State," "Religion and
Education," and "Religion and Family" were discussed, as well as
the August 1991 Christian-Muslim meeting in Ibadan, Nigeria, on
"Cooperation in Human Development" organized by the Pontifical
Council for Inter-Religious Dialogue. Noteworthy also is the fact that
Christians and Muslims in South Africa, as members of the World
Conference on Religion and Peace, joined hands to struggle against
apartheid.

   Christ said to his disciples: "You shall be my witnesses to the
end of the earth." Actually, commitment to service in society, striving for authentic Christian unity, working together with Muslims
for the establishment of peace and justice, can all be considered
as Christian witness, along with Christian songs, Christian marriage
and family life, intercessory prayer for Muslims, telling the story of
Jesus, and so on. In this way, we will be instruments in the hands of
our Lord Jesus Christ, who continues to draw human beings to himself, from all nations and communities in this world. May his name
be praised forever.

Postscript

Vision and Hope

Desmond Tutu

If you lived on another planet and you were traveling in your flying
saucer scouting around for another planet to which you wanted to
emigrate, our planet Earth would almost certainly be way down in
the popularity stakes. It has had two world wars in this one century
and numerous other wars since. Just look at it now—there has been
the Gulf War, the awfulness of conflict in Yugoslavia, the carnage
in Sri Lanka, the injustices and oppression in Latin America, and the
strife in the Middle East.

In addition there have been devastating earthquakes and floods
in one place and equally devastating droughts in another. You might
have thought that God could have arranged things slightly better so
that there was, for example, enough water to go around for everybody, instead of too much in one place and none in another. There
have been excesses, corruption, abuse of power here, there, and
everywhere. It has all in many ways been the worst possible ad-
vertisement for the belief that there is a good, benevolent, and
all-powerful God at the control of things in our universe. Surely, the
evidence seems to point in the opposite direction.

I have a beautiful book of cartoons entitled *My God*. One shows
God contemplating contradictory appeals and prayers from human
creatures on earth, and God says feelingly, "I wish I could say, 'Don't
call me, I'll call you!' " But the two I really want to refer to show,
first, God looking glum and saying, "Create in six days and have eternity to regret it," and second, God quite disconsolate, declaring, "I
think I have lost my copy of the divine plan." Those say it all. Looking at the state of the world, you might be forgiven for wondering
if God had any plan at all.

The Most Rev. Desmond Tutu is archbishop of the Anglican Church of Southern Africa
and president of the All Africa Conference of Churches. This is an edited version of
his reflection at the pre-Assembly meeting of the South Africa Council of Churches in
Johannesburg in June 1992. It was printed in *The Source* (vol. 1, no. 3), the bulletin
of the Sixth General Assembly of the AACC.

And I have not even mentioned Africa in this doleful picture. Our people have had a horrible raw deal. When people from other parts of the world wanted slaves, it was to Africa that they came for what seemed to be an inexhaustible supply. When European imperialists were carving up the world, Africa did not escape this chauvinist predatory exercise referred to as the "scramble for Africa." It was carved up with scant attention to where colonial boundaries were drawn, so that people who belonged to the same tribe ended up on opposite sides of the boundary lines. Africa was exploited for the benefit of those who called the tune in the imperial and colonial capitals. With breathtaking arrogance, Africa's history, culture, religion, and way of life were undermined and, in many places, virtually destroyed.

"How Long, O Lord?"

The people were calling out, "How long, O Lord? God, where are you?" As God seemed so stubbornly absent, deaf, or blind, they asked, "God, on whose side are you?" As God seemed so unequivocally on the side of the strong, the callous, and totally unprincipled ones, our people all over looked longingly to the day when they would walk tall and unfettered in liberated and independent countries. The end of colonialism and imperialism came and there was jubilation and ecstasy as first one and then another and yet another African country became independent and free.

Alas, it was all to be short-lived, for all that seemed to have changed for God's so-called ordinary people was the color of the oppressor. Formerly it had been the white colonial ruler who had his foot on their neck. Now it became their own flesh and blood who became the oppressor and the exploiter. We know just how appalling the human rights record has become in Africa. There has been less freedom in independent Africa than during the much-maligned colonial period.

There was a virtual orgy of totalitarian military dictatorships and their accompanying spate of coups. An elite creamed off the resources of their motherland as they enriched themselves in an uncontrollable spree of corruption and inefficiency. As a result, our continent groans under an enormous foreign debt burden of US $270 billion.

Africa is devastated by drought and famine but also by totally unnecessary wars that have gulped down untold millions of dollars, wantonly wasted on arms and instruments of death and destruction.

The catalog of Africa's wars within and between countries is doleful and quite shattering – Liberia, Sudan, Somalia, Togo, Burundi, Mozambique, Angola. Perhaps one could say more easily where there is no fighting, for now there is strife in Egypt and Nigeria.

Africa has over 50 percent of the world's refugee population (7.5 million) and the Organization of African Unity secretary general says there are another 10 million "displaced persons." Infant mortality is unacceptably high, illiteracy is a bane, health care is not readily available to all, many do not have water, and the standard of living is appallingly low. It is a mockery to speak about abundant life – and yet, is it?

How can we speak about abundant life when in addition to all the woes described we have to add the specter of AIDS? Yes, we can speak about abundant life, for Jesus Christ has overcome darkness and evil. Through his glorious resurrection he won a great victory on the cross, so that we can say that evil and death and injustice and oppression cannot have the last word, do not have the last word.

Is it not amazing that after all these years of repression and blatant disregard for human rights, when people have been harassed, tortured, imprisoned, and assassinated for standing for the truth, when dictators have seemed so thoroughly entrenched, that God's people could refuse to acquiesce in their being dehumanized? Isn't it a glorious saga of the eruption of freedom in so many and such unlikely places? Hey man, this is indeed God's world and God is in charge. This is God's world and God cares about evil and oppression and injustice. Dictators thought that they were firmly in the saddle and, unbelievably to them, they are biting the dust everywhere.

Perfect Freedom

People are demonstrating that they have been created freely for freedom. An unfree human being is a contradiction in terms. God, who alone has the perfect right to be a totalitarian, has such a deep reverence for our fundamental freedom to be persons that God would much rather see us go freely to hell than compel us to go to heaven.

It is impossible for injustice and oppression and evil to prevail forever. That is what we used to say here in the darkest hour of our apartheid agony. We used to say to our oppressors, "Hey, watch it. You're not God. We are being nice to you. We invite you to join the winning side, for you have already lost. If you choose injustice and evil and oppression, then you are taking on God, and you've had it."

It is God's dream that all His children must live harmoniously together. It is God's dream that we must live, not just survive. It is
God's dream that we appropriate the gift of abundant life that God
has made available in Jesus Christ. We must tell it on the mountains
that South Africa will be a beautiful land when all corruption will
have ended; when the government won't budget, as this year it has,
five billion rand for covert activities, which in the past included the
assassination of its opponents. Can you imagine how many schools,
clinics, and homes could be built with five billion rand?

South Africa will become a beautiful land when the government
is accountable to the people and there won't be those who foment
violence so that others can gloat about what they call black-on-black
violence; when the government of the people will ensure that there
is security for all, that health care and education and housing and
clean water and clean air will be accessible to all, and all will live
full and productive lives. And God will look on and rub His hands
in satisfaction and declare that all that He made was not just good,
but very good.